IN – BETWEEN PLACES

IN-BETWEEN PLACES

ESSAYS BY DIANE GLANCY

The University of Arizona Press   Tucson

The University of Arizona Press
© 2005 Diane Glancy

∞ This book is printed on acid-free, archival-quality paper.
Manufactured in the United States of America

10   09   08   07   06   05   6   5   4   3   2   1

Library of Congress Cataloging-in-Publication Data
Glancy, Diane.
In-between places: essays / by Diane Glancy.
p.   cm.
ISBN 0-8165-2385-1 (alk. paper)—ISBN 0-8165-2387-8 (pbk: alk. paper)
1. Glancy, Diane.   2. Place (Philosophy) in literature.
3. Landscape in literature.   I. Title.
PS3557.L294I5   2004
814'.54—dc22
2004001863

Publication of this book is made possible in part by the proceeds of a permanent
endowment created with the assistance of a Challenge Grant from the National
Endowment for the Humanities, a federal agency.

For my father, Lewis Hall,
my brother and sister-in-law, David and Jan Hall,
my son and daughter-in-law, David and Angie Glancy,
and my grandsons, Joseph and Charles Brouillette.

For my daughter and son-in-law, Jennifer and Scott Brouillette,
my granddaughter, Elizabeth Ann Brouillette,
and my maternal grandmother, Anna Myrtle Adams Wood.

CONTENTS

Written language seems to me a landscape. Land bound up in words. I pick up stones or rocks in travel as texts that I can read.

There is a map you open like a book. There are books you open like a map.

There is a map you decide to call a book. A book of the territories you've traveled. A book of the in–between places you've lived. A map is a meaning you hold against the unknowing. The places you speak in many directions.

A map is a potholder for the geographies of the land and the language it carries.

INTRODUCTION

IN–BETWEEN PLACES

JULY

She Has Some Potholders

. . . a pattern I remembered / from odd pieces of an old family quilt. / Then bringing it finally back against / the darkness of my cheek
> July, "The Book of Lowilva"
> *What Nature,* Steve Fay

I AM A week and a half into teaching Native American literature and fiction writing in the Bread Loaf–New Mexico program when I realize it is going to be more work than I had expected. I spend all winter in classrooms. Why did I agree to teach again in the summer? In the evenings, the students go to a roadhouse named El Alto, but I have to make comments on student stories and read assigned stories from *Sudden Fiction* and *The Best American Short Stories.* Even after that, it takes a while to go to sleep.

I am staying in the River House at the end of a dirt road overlooking the Pecos River on the edge of the Native American Preparatory School campus. It is a long, low, spacious house built into the hill. The land is still a pale green because there has been rain, but the heat is rising. The piñon and fir, cedar, pine, spruce, and juniper are a darker green. I smelled the piñon as soon as I turned north on New Mexico Highway 84 from Interstate 40.

Outside the River House there's a small courtyard with four small aspen trees against a red adobe wall. In the mornings, I watch the shade under the honeysuckle, the blooms of squash, trumpet vine, maybe lavender. Those flowers I don't know.

I like the southwestern architecture: the beamed ceilings, carved doors, and tile. The beehive fireplaces in each room for the chilly nights. I have the headmaster's house, called the River House; I have two rooms, one for sleeping, one for working. There's a gathering room, a kitchen, and then the rest of the house below. Inside the front door, in a large inset window, there is a statue of a stylized woman, nearly life-sized, with the quarter moon looking up her skirt. There is an old native myth—when the sun was female, and the moon, male—warning against incest, and I wonder if it is behind the meaning of the statue. There are other artifacts and paintings in the River House (the reason they asked me to keep it locked). Also in the long hallway there's a birchbark canoe probably made by students at the Native American Preparatory School.

The first thing I hear is that there are a lot of mice this year, which means a lot of rattlesnakes. I walk to the eating hall watching for them. I feel the sun as I walk uphill, soon out of breath in the 7,000-foot altitude.

July is the seventh month of the year. It has thirty-one days. July comes from the Roman calendar month Julius (after Julius Caesar). The month Julius was formerly Quintilius. Julius received its name in 44 BC. Julius was (formerly) the fifth month of the year. July is now the attic of the year. July is temperature. Fever. Skillet. Fry. July is landscape. July is a map of the landscape. July is blueprint. July is sheet music. July spelled backwards spells yluJ. *Iluge. Illusionate.* To make illusions of. July needs a potholder, which writing is. A friend, Anne Kingsbury, a fabric artist and owner of the Woodland Pattern Bookstore in Milwaukee, made a series of potholders and called them the Autobiographical Potholder Series. I want to borrow the idea for writing. This July, particularly, needs a potholder.

They say rain will come soon. They call it the monsoon season. Already there are short bursts of rain in the afternoons. Afterwards, it is cooler for a while.

In the Native American literature course, we are reading *Native American Literature: An Anthology,* Lawana Trout, editor, NTC Publishing Group, Lincolnwood, Illinois, 1999, 777 pages. There are questions: What is an Indian? What is literature? Why is this particular literature uncomfortable? (The students want to read other books, and I add Sherman Alexie's *The Lone Ranger and Tonto Fist Fight in Heaven* to the reading list.) How do we get beyond stereotype and romanticism? What do we live for? Where does evil come from?

The easy question first: You get beyond idealization by reading the diverse voices in the anthology, from Elias Boudinot (Cherokee), who argued for assimilation in 1826, to Debra Calling Thunder (Arapaho), who wrote about traditional life. Boudinot: "There are three things of late occurrence. First: The invention of letters. Second. The translation of the New Testament into Cherokee. And Third. The organization of a Government" (195). Calling Thunder: "The buffalo sang to us, and their song was our life—The buffalo sang to us so that we would grow strong. And the Old People would gather together many words to make prayers to the Creator. They would gather words as they walked a sacred path across the Earth, leaving nothing behind but prayers and offerings" (228). How can you reconcile the differing Indian voices?

It is the same with the other voices in the same chapter (in the whole book, for that matter): Yellow Wolf (Nez Perce), after a vision quest, 1869: "It was the Spirit of a wolf that appeared to me. Yellowlike in color, it sort of floated in the air. Like a human being it talked to me. And gave me its power" (244). Charles Eastman (Santee Sioux), after witnessing the massacre at Wounded Knee, 1891: "All this was a severe ordeal for one who had so lately put all his faith in the Christian love and lofty ideals of the white man" (274).

Between 1789 and 1871, there were 370 treaties made, according to Trout (186).

A few historical events:

1838   *Trail of Tears (Cherokee) (on which Boudinot walked)*
1864   *Long Walk (Navajo) to Fort Sumner*
1864   *Sand Creek Massacre in Colorado (Colonel Chivington attacked the Southern Cheyenne and Arapaho)*
1868   *Washita River in Oklahoma (Cheyenne) (General Custer and the Seventh Cavalry attacked Black Kettle's encampment)*
1876   *Little Big Horn in Montana (Custer and the Seventh Cavalry were massacred)*
1877   *Bear Paw Battlefield in Montana (Nez Perce) (Chief Joseph defeated by General Sherman)*
1890   *Wounded Knee in South Dakota (Dakota) (the Seventh Cavalry massacred Big Foot's band)*

I move to the next easiest questions: What is literature? My travel dictionary, Webster's *School & Office,* defines it as a body of writing with merit, without defining merit, but I suppose it means the use of literary technique, character, plot, and theme effectively, until all the parts transcend some human condition.

Trout calls her book *Native American Literature,* but it's a historical document, one of the students says, it just repeats the myths without the voice, the drama. It doesn't live, like Ovid's *Metamorphosis.* There's no author here. Well, sometimes there is. Some of the pieces are livelier than others. But the students want to read novels. I say, "Can't you see this anthology as many voices in relationship to others, telling a complicated and diverse story of a people that were here when the Spaniards and other Europeans came? Can you see it as a process of recovery? Can you see it as stories through their own words? A containment of the heart, which would otherwise be lost in grief. Broken and unentertaining as life is itself sometimes. Can you change your expectations? Knowing that the meaning of yourself is bound up in the meaning you find in the literature?"

Now the questions I'm not sure how to address: What do we live for? According to the fundamental Bible belt, to make a decision for Jesus Christ. In a traditional Indian way, it is to survive, to struggle for survivance (Gerald Vizenor's word, which is survival with meaning), to move from being a human being to a Human Being with responsibility to one's family, tribe, and land.

You see, there are always opposite roads to follow. One toward a knowledge of Christ (who is a person, a living being, not a denomination); the other toward an understanding of the way a heritage has worked: a reciprocity in the relational working of the universe.

Maybe it is tied in with the hardest question. Where does evil come from? It seems to be inbred. It seems to come from inside. I am born with a self-will that is defiant to the existence of God. Whatever evil is—it seems to differ between denominations. In Catholicism (though I am not Catholic) there are seven deadly sins—and maybe an eighth, not belonging to the Catholic Church (which results in damnation). In fundamental (non-Catholic) Christianity, there is one: blasphemy of the Holy Spirit, which is unbelief (meaning not believing Christ died on the cross for my sins, which has nothing to do with the church).

It is about a relationship with Christ without the trappings of denominations.

Do good and evil exist as opposite forces? Are they two parts of the same? Is evil relative? An energy force that is sometimes good and bad, and should not be separated or judged as good or bad?

Most Indians don't believe in evil. But ask about their *conquest,* as Trout calls it, their *extermination.* Was that an evil done to them? Certainly not in the opinion of the Seventh Cavalry.

And what about taboos? This you cannot do. It is wrong. Where does the will to do that wrong come from?

In Christianity, Satan was an angel of light who thought himself so handsome he could be God—so he persuaded some other angels to rebel against God.

He was overthrown, cast out of heaven, and came to earth to cause havoc with God's new creation. He tempted Eve to eat the apple (use her own judgment) and was *delegged*. According to Christianity, the serpent's poison is still with us.

But where did Satan's problem come from? Pride? Thinking of himself as above the living God? Self-centeredness? Setting self, or the awareness of self, apart from (above) others? It was the free will that said, *"I can be God."* In the native community, others always come before self. There is something puzzling about the Christian God who allows free will, self-will, even to the point of self-destruction or destruction of others.

There are dichotomies, inconsistencies, conflicts, inherent contradictions in every culture. In Christianity itself. When Israel crossed the Red Sea and entered the land of Canaan, it was full of tribes: the Canaanites, Hittites, Perizzites. Israel had God's blessing in exterminating those peoples of the land, even women, children, and animals. This God of love, mercy, justice. The European immigrants felt they could do the same to the Indians.

Well, welcome to the literature and the discussion of questions that arise. I don't have many answers here. Nothing is simple. Not much is clear. You will be as uncomfortable as I am.

My memories of July are something like darkness in which there is a large, square tree, a pinwheel spinning on it; my father had nailed it there. It was the July Fourth by which all other July Fourths would fizzle, a pinhole through which all July Fourths would spin. Even later, at huge fireworks shows, it was in the yard of our small house in Kansas City where the definitive Fourth took place. July Fourth is only one day of July, but it is the loop on the corner of the potholder. My father was the center. This is for you, Father (dead over thirty years now); this July is still yours.

Usually, I'm at my brother's place on the Lake of the Ozarks in Missouri for the Fourth. This year, I go to Laguna Pueblo for a feast day and the three hundredth anniversary of the mission. It is a 2½ hour drive from the Native American Preparatory School near Rowe, south on Interstate 25, past Albuquerque to Laguna on Interstate 40 West. I watch the dancers in the plaza, go inside the mission church on the hill, eat, walk past the booths, return to the school.

That night, I stand on the balcony of the River House and see the fireworks over the hills in the distance. I think of the contradiction in celebrating July Fourth at an Indian pueblo. I think of what the country's independence meant to the Native American. As Muriel Rukeyser says in *The Life of Poetry*, *"that most excellent invention, America."*

It seems right I spend winter in Minnesota, summer in New Mexico.

I'm still reading for the Native American literature class in the afternoon. I will be reading the anthology all summer.

As I walk up the hot and steep dirt road to the eating hall, I see dark clouds to the south. I ignore them. The monsoon season in such an arid climate seems unlikely. Each day I roll down the windows of the car as it sits at the River House because of the heat. I am eating lunch when the storm breaks loose. It rains for nearly an hour. Torrents. Hail. Reddish brown water rushes in the arroyo by the eating hall. I think of my car with its open windows, parked at the River House. I wait until 2:00, time for my class to meet. We've started meeting in the River House because the room where we were scheduled was too hot. I see a student coming up the walk. He asks if I need a ride. Everyone is waiting at the River House.

I talk about what I've written. The questions asked during the last class that I've tried to answer. The students read from various sections of chapter 4. I get through the Trail of Tears, the massacre of Black Kettle at the Washita River in Oklahoma, Sand Creek, but when a student reads how during the Long March, the soldiers killed the sheep in front of the Navajo, I begin to cry. It continues from time to time as students read of Chief Joseph in Montana and Wounded Knee in South Dakota. My father worked in the stockyards. I'm used to the slaughter of animals. What's the matter with me?

I've always had the propensity to cry. My mother said as a baby I cried a lot. I remember at a Campfire Girl camp, I cried when rain covered the road and we were stranded for longer than necessary. It was the first time I remember the overwhelming sense of sadness and loss. What I was, wasn't there. I have felt that inexplicable grief all my life. Maybe open grief keeps you humble. It is something I hate to do: be swallowed by emotion.

I feel this class will not go well. They want camaraderie. They want references to theorists who do not consider the native viewpoint. They want to see *Other* in their own way. They want a conclusion toward which they can move. They want what they want in the way they want it. A *Bread Loaf summer,* as one student says. But the direction is away from unity. We're headed toward the morass of figuring out native life. I also have a well-educated young Indian student. The class looks to him for answers I don't have. And he has them. My way will be a difficult, non-closured, *UnBread Loaf summer* of maybe things running their own way, asking questions for which there are no easy answers, maybe not even answers. Dragging you in, letting you out with nothing except what you construct for yourself. I want to continue with that *lesson plan.* I would withdraw if I could. Head back north to Minnesota. Anywhere but here.

After class, I take the floor mats out of my car and try to soak up the water with towels. It will take a while to dry out. I leave the windows down, but soon it is pouring again. That night, I drive up the hill to the Monday night movies in the main building, the car is fogged up because of all the wetness inside.

I wake at 4:00 in the morning. Something is in the room. I listen and soon I hear it again. I turn on the light, sit up. It's a mouse running around the edge of the room. It runs under the bed. When I look for it, I see the bottom of the box spring is torn. The mouse is hiding somewhere in the bed. I get my pillow and clock and move to the other room, but don't sleep again.

That morning, two mice are running up and down the hall, having a good time, eating and drinking like Job's sons and daughters before the wind blows their house down upon them. At breakfast, I ask for a mousetrap.

I come back to the River House and work.

In the afternoon, I teach my classes as a community. The students are responsible for presenting some of the chapters in Native American literature, and some of the stories and writing exercises in fiction.

I also want to think about what I'm working on, because I have to hold to it or be flung into disorder and nothingness. I've been wrapped up in fiction. I want to write poetry also, which resides in another space than fiction. Someone in class said that poetry is looking at the negative of a photograph; therefore, fiction must be the photograph itself. Or maybe poetry is the potholder between the handles of the bowl and the hands.

When I return from classes, the whole meadow to the River House is stove-hot midday. In the evening, when the sun is not directly overhead, the road is more beige than white hot.

I have fourteen papers to read and grade for the Native American literature class. Beside grades, we are required to turn in a single-spaced page of written comments on each student. There are approximately seventy students at the Bread Loaf School of English. They are mainly high school teachers working on their master's degrees.

When the class is over, the weekend opens up and I feel a vast loneliness, though I will be busy with work all weekend. I have twelve stories along with the papers to grade and make comments on, plus getting reading done for classes the next week. I have always liked to be by myself anyway. I remember driving some-place once, and my former husband said, *you didn't say a word the whole trip.* I like it when I'm the only one on the road.

Tonight, students have invited some of the faculty to a roadhouse. *El Alto.* When I ask how to get there, they say I will get there if I'm meant to show up. I drive there with two other faculty who know where the place is. I like the young men. They shoot pool and show me how to chalk the stick and hit a ball. The rest of the time I watch. About midnight, I drive 2.7 miles on the dirt road from the inter-state to the Native American Preparatory School for the first time after dark, and follow the turns, the ups and downs of the hills.

One morning, I walk up the hill to the eating hall for breakfast. There is a herd of cows in the meadow that climbs upward from the Pecos to the main part of the campus. I feel like I am in the stockyards where my father worked. As I walk through them; the mothers moo to their calves to get up from resting at the side of the road where I pass. The calves stand and run to their mothers. I also no-tice—what is it—with horns? A bull? Yes. I see him watching from the corner of my eye. It is a bull. *How territorial are they?* I ask in the eating hall. No, he won't charge, they say. But as I walk back to the River House, the men from the Native American Preparatory School arrive in their trucks to herd the cows, calves, and bull back across the Pecos.

The student who is staying in my house in St. Paul to take care of my cat sends the mail and some calls I have to answer. I look forward to what she sends in a manila envelope. Bills and business, mainly, and a review of my new book. I read papers all morning, walk up the steep hill to the eating hall for lunch. It rains all afternoon as I grade papers.

"It should not be news to any writer that *all* writing involves ordering, shaping, selecting and omitting details. In ordering, we distort the facts, but not necessarily the truth" "On the Need for the Lie" (an article in *Minnesota Literature,* February 1999), by W. Scott Olsen.

I want to think about the representation of real/unreal until the real is subverted without evidence of the subversion. Nor is it apparent what the unreal is, because it is made to seem real. I have wanted to be with these ideas.

What is Indian identity? Certainly, involvement with the culture. But when you give up the culture, as my father did, it does not leave, though you live far from the Indian community and are actually uncomfortable with it. You feel yourself an outsider. Like someone you used to date and left without explanation; you feel you still owe him something.

Indian identity also is the evidence of the existence of subversion because the Indian text is found between disputes: the vertical reality of white culture on orbiculate native thought, and the pull of native thought on a linear world.

Down there by the Pecos, where I'm listening at this moment, I hear the resistance of the rocks in the stream. One of the reasons for the resistance is the passage of one text over another, the moving and unmoving, with the subtext of the migration. The poetics of essay is the same flight across the boundaries: a transference of abstract poetics, not as in poetry, but as in the shape of prose.

The beginning of the world is a voice *speaking into being*. A geography of language.

Now comes the part of Olsen's article I don't agree with: "We're asking our words to stand for something larger. At that level, we're all lying, and I think that's okay." It's not the okay part, but asking our words to stand for something larger. That's what they're supposed to do. Therein is the truth of words that we can't get at without them.

As Lyn Hejinian writes in the introduction to *The Language of Inquiry*, "poetry can turn language upon itself and thus exceed its own limits."

I heard William Heyen speak at a conference earlier in the summer in Atlanta. It was one of the stops I made on my way to New Mexico. He talked over and over about how poetry was the language of things that can't be gotten to. It lives in the in-between places.

I look over the notes I took: Follow a poem by its sound. Sound is a guide to what comes next. A clue toward forward motion. Sound is a pool where we get into the earliest mind (to get us back to the beginning—that original awe). The sound we follow back to ourselves (to find out what we know).

We can't write with our upper mind, Heyen continued. That's where essays are written. Poetry gets into the mind unconsciously, as if in a semi-trance. Heyen says he seeks the bottomless poem.

I often think this is the place I want to be. It is being in touch with what is. As a horse is a spirit horse. *"What does that mean?"* Heyen asked. Someone had talked to him about the term. But it is *sacred,* not spirit, horse. It comes from the same indirect path that poetry does. Or something like poetry is come upon when the real self connects to an otherness that moves with words into the *that which is* where it can turn. Pulled back to say *this is the way, this is it.* It is a sacred consciousness. It is what is lost in the upper mind. It is what America pushed out of the way: the sacredness, the horse, the animals, the land, the understanding of that place where they began, the people on it.

A man named Emilio Arauxo from Galicia (Spain), that land of troubadours, as he calls it, e-mailed me before I left St. Paul. He asked some questions about poetry, which I answered. Now he writes a letter with six more questions about poetry, which I like:

1.   What is your experience of the language? Does the poem invent another language inside the language?

I think language places us in the world. Language is the land on which I live. There is a Native American belief that our stories can't be separated from the land, but in the case of the Cherokee, who were removed from the original place of their stories in the Southeast and forced to march west on the 1838 Trail of Tears, something else has to occur: a belief that either stories move also or that we carry them within us; in other words, the land is an attitude or place located in the mind. The geography of thought. Otherwise, we are left without stories.

Yes, there is another language inside the language of the poem. I have already mentioned it: It is a geographical location in the abstract; the abstraction of landscape which the language of the poem establishes and attaches itself to.

2. And what would you say of the function of poetry? Is poetry like cure, repair, liturgy, exorcism, revelation, charm, thought—?

    Charm is my favorite of the above words. Like calling a python from its basket by the magic of voice (instead of flute). All the evils come out and dance. By evils, I mean the mundane and unmagical that is charmed into a balance with sound.

3. And how does poetry express nature, landscape, or even the country? How does poetry express space?

    By having its being in space—the space of the page on which its written. The space of the spoken word as it travels from the mouth to the ear of another and creates a new space in the mind.

4. What is the role of experience and experimentation in your poetry?

    I think I write from experience—ordinary experience—the struggle to get to that other meaning that lives on the other side of the hill from fiction. I feel experimentation is important because it captures the fragmentation of native experience.

5.   And what solution do you contribute to the integration of the other
      arts in poetry?

      I believe in the music of the sound of words and in the visual art of
      imagery the words make. I think I contribute to the understanding of the
      mixed-blood, assimilated voice. I try to get away from romanticizing na-
      tive life. I have known the plainness of it, yet I come away transfixed.

6.   Does the poem stand alone with its mystery?

      Yes.

I have not seen any snakes, but this morning, as I start down the hill on my way
back from the eating hall, I see a rattlesnake crossing the road. I stop. Back up
slowly. He is brown, probably three to four feet long. At the top of the hill, a small
dirt road goes to the left, to the laundry building, and there's another road from
it down to the River House, forming a large triangle around the snake stretched
across the road. I take it, singing my snake song. Maybe the translation is something like this: *I am walking down the dirt road. Snake, I know the road is yours. You*
come for the mice that run into my house. Snake, I honor you as mouse-eater. I do not
want your poison bite. shh shh suu suu shuus shuh shua. I see a small wet place on the
road. Is that where you've been? Don't you have crops to tend? Maybe your lovely wife is
calling—Don't you have your water jug to fill at the Pecos?

      Later, I look in a book, *Easy Field Guide to Southwestern Snakes,* that another
faculty member gave me because two years ago, the woman staying in the River
House found a rattlesnake in the bathroom. The faculty member thinks this is
funny. There are eight choices for the rattlesnake I bypassed at a distance: western
diamondback, Mojave, blacktail, tiger, rock, twin-spotted, ridgenose, western.
The snake was brown with diamond-shaped spots. I would say it was a western
diamondback or a Mojave, which the book says "are similar in appearance."

      I think the snake was daydreaming as he crossed the road. He just ambled
slowly on as I backed away at some distance.

I wonder what to tie Native American literature to—what tag to place on it. (My new car tags just arrived with other mail in a large manila envelope. My license plate: BLZ 949. BLZ for a Minnesota blizzard.) What critical framework to put around it. But I feel a resistance. In class, a student asked about Edward Said. But I didn't know what to say. What did Said say about the Native American? In *Culture and Imperialism,* he states, "We have to concede that as an immigrant settler society superimposed on the ruins of considerable native presence, American identity is too varied to be a unitary and homogenous thing" (xxv). On page 63 of the same book, Said mentions the "wholesale colonization and destruction of Native American life."

But native life still exists, as does the Native American. Native American literature is postcolonial, to be sure. Postmodern also. It has felt the stranglehold of imperialism, but the culture is more than ruins. It is more than nonexistent. It is a varied and vital culture with multiple beginnings and multiple directions.

Maybe Native American literature could begin with no point of reference. Well, everything comes from somewhere. But I like to think of the literature as self-referential (with a reason). Beginning in itself. I think it also wants to define itself, be itself without any outside definition of what it is, or should be. I am going to let the literature speak for itself this summer. I do not want other voices shedding their *light* on our *darkness.*

"I speak many languages. I discuss many things," Raven says in chapter 7 of *Native American Literature: An Anthology* (Trout), in the James Welch piece, "The Marriage of Red Paint and White Man's Dog" from his historical novel *Fools Crow.* I don't know the difference between ravens and crows, but two crows (or ravens) have flown over the valley above the Pecos since I arrived. They sit on the roof outside the deck of the lower bedroom and squawk. Sometimes I speak to them. "I even speak with the swift silver people who live in the water," Raven says (567), "but they are dumb."

Two colleagues tell me how the crows had a metal ring of some sort and fought over it on the roof early one morning. The one colleague says when she looked up through the skylight, the crows looked down at her.

"They're doing it for you," I tell her. "They watch us. They've seen the basketball games on the court. They can play too."

The crow is an old Trickster, an observer, a mimic. He shows us ourselves. He walks on the ground like a single-engine plane hopping over a bumpy field, until his black wings spread and he flaps into the air. A coal-black savior, his wings outstretched to the sky.

The whole country was lighted by a searing light with the intensity many times that of the midday sun.
    —Brig. Gen. Thomas Farrel

The Trinity Site at the White Sands Missile Range is four hours south on I-25 from the Native American Preparatory School. My Ford Taurus turns 98,000 miles on the trip. We stop first at the Atomic Energy Museum at Kirtland Air Force Base in Albuquerque. At the museum we see a military film full of smugness and back-patting for pulling it off (developing the thought in Einstein's Theory of Relativity that something more could come from something less). In the film, I hear the old American newsreel bravado I remember from the '50s when America could do no wrong. "We tricked them," the guide says. "They thought the *Enola Gay* was just another U.S. weather plane that made a daily flight over Japan."

I was born before Pearl Harbor. I was a small child when America entered World War II. There are forces that cannot be appeased. Hitler's Germany, for instance. Other countries stepped into the war until the United States dropped the bomb on Hiroshima and Nagasaki. Many of the men in my family have been involved in war. I was too young to understand that the country was at war, but I must have picked up some of the worry and anxiety. For some reason, my mother decided to visit her sister in San Francisco during the blackout days. I wonder now if it could have been difficulty between her and my father, though they stayed married all their lives. We left Kansas City in the middle of the country and traveled by train to the West Coast. Something in our lives was torn up. There were nightmares. The fear of enemy attack. I fell down the steps of the train at a stop in Nevada and nearly cut the right side of my nose from my face. I think I had already burned my legs. I had yet to jump up in a chair and fall headfirst through the glass door of a bookcase in our living room. My mother could not nurture in the way I needed. I was a stranger in an unsettled house. I was stupid. I was smart. I remember it as if stranded on some distant beach where I would be for life. Yet a spirit came up through the earth as I played. Little jolts of recognition of something beyond the something.

From Albuquerque, we continue south past Socorro and exit I-25 at Highway 380. We follow the road for about seventeen miles to the Stallion Gate of the White Sands Missile Range. We show car registration and insurance at the checkpoint. After some instructions and the signing of a waiver that says we realize this is a missile range and there are missiles and explosives in the area and the government is not responsible if we get hurt, we follow the guide in an official U.S. government vehicle (a pewter Suburban).

The 51,500-acre area was declared a national historic landmark in 1975.

Trinity (ground zero) is a large, fenced circle. In the center is an obelisk (just taller than a man) made of volcanic rock.

On the ground there are still the remains of trinitite, which is desert sand turned into a green, glassy rock from the heat of the blast. Most of it was cleaned up, but bits of it remain. "Do not pick it up." The guide has given us a booklet. "It is still radioactive."

"The story of Trinity Site begins with the formation of the Manhattan Project, formed in June 1942." The project was actually international. There were several Nobel Prize winners who came to America from Italy and Germany, fleeing Hitler and Mussolini, including, of course, Einstein with his $E = MC^2$.

The project also was national. The booklet the guide has given us says, "At Oak Ridge, Tennessee, huge gas diffusion and electromagnetic process plants were built to separate uranium 235 from its more common form, uranium 238. Hanford, Washington, became the home for nuclear reactors which produced a new element called plutonium. Los Alamos was established to design and build the bomb. At Los Alamos many of the greatest scientific minds labored over the theory and actual construction of the device." (And of course, in the South Pacific, pilots were practicing how to drop the bomb and make a quick turnaround—this was from the film at the Atomic Energy Museum.)

"In an atomic explosion, a chain reaction picks up speed as atoms split, releasing neutrons plus great amounts of energy. The escaping neutrons strike and split more atoms, thus releasing more neutrons and energy. In a nuclear explosion this all occurs in a millionth of a second with billions of atoms being split."

"Trinity Site is where the first atomic bomb was tested at 5:29:45 a.m. Mountain War Time on July 16, 1945. The 19 kiloton explosion not only led to a quick end to the war in the Pacific but also ushered the world into the atomic age. All life on Earth has been touched by the event which took place here."

A few weeks later, Hiroshima. And because the Japanese still wouldn't surrender, Nagasaki three days later.

It was a thoughtful, sobering trip—eerie, puzzling—with the usual inherent contradictions that can be pulled out of anything significant. Was it worth it after all? (Not the trip, but the dropping of the bomb.) What would have happened if the bomb had not been used?—maybe never even developed? (Which seems as pointless as asking, What if the white man hadn't come?) We are on our way into the new (nuclear) age—we are always going to be on our way—that's what humankind is about—and we stood on the spot where it was ushered in. As one participant said, "This is the closest I've been to hell."

July seventeenth, my brother's birthday; he was born in 1944, mid–WW II, while an uncle was in France. I remember my mother at the curb sixty years ago, getting into the car, heavy with the weight of my brother, when it was time for him to be born.

"North American," my brother says when I call. He's a meat broker who works from his phone on the Lake of the Ozarks in Missouri. He sells carcasses of beef. He's a middleman.

There's the leg of a small animal in the road as I walk up to the eating hall for breakfast. I am reminded again of that violent country of nature.

It rains all evening. One of the skylights in the River House drips into a plant holder on legs, which is tin. The roof is peaked, and the plant holder is in a corner that goes from the bottom floor to the ceiling. There is a loud plop with each drop.

I am reading a book, *From the Heart of the Country,* by J. M. Coetzee, which I found in the Bread Loaf–New Mexico library. I also read Coetzee's *The Lives of Animals.*

Once in Texas after visiting my son, I passed a truck and horse trailer. Ahead, I pulled into a rest stop, and as I got out of the car, the truck and trailer passed, and I heard a *bang, bang.* The horse was kicking its foot against the trailer, wanting out. I feel that bang. That *horse wanting out.* I wanted out of my isolation also. I was at a distance from both heritages. My father's buried native culture, my mother's European heritage.

My son has a horse named Zeke who snorts when he's hungry, acts over-worked when he's ridden. An animal should have a place to be itself.

If I had a man, he would have to be a traveling man. A road man (I had listened to Borges' "Yard Master" in his *Selected Fictions* as I drove through Oklahoma on my way to New Mexico for the summer).

Yes. "70 percent of the Native American class is mad at you," a student says. "I would call it more like 100 percent," I answer. Now I have a conference with each student. Toward the end of class (the class after I turned back their papers) they announce they've talked among themselves. They feel I graded them too hard. I wasn't clear on what I wanted.

These are the grades they are disgruntled about: A (1), A– (1), B+ (4), B (4), B– (4). I had told them I would leave the paper content open. They could write about what they wanted to write about. I would like it to link somehow with the literature we've read in class. This is a literature course.

They say they feel set up. I gave them freedom, then marked them down when their papers didn't link to the literature, or they were redundant in talking about their own sense of identity/heritage/culture, or the parts of their paper didn't hold together for me, or they didn't synthesize the different parts, or whatever.

This is the cool, "in" group at Bread Loaf–New Mexico. You can tell. Young men in their late twenties and three young women. So now papers are due again at the end of the coming week. This time I am more specific. Around the borders of the potholder it is written:

PAPER #2 NATIVE AMERICAN LITERATURE

Again, I want four pages (because of the compressed nature of this summer session), titled, numbered, double-spaced.

I want to see a sense of discovery,
a point reached,
a connection made to otherness (defined in your own terms).

I want to see information disseminated into your own work and in your own words.
I want to find structural completeness from the beginning to end.
All directions should point to the center (the theme).
All disharmony (imbalance) should be in harmony (unless you define the purpose of the disharmony).

Be experimental and risky if you wish.

I want to feel a connection or recognition of something you've come across in your thinking during readings or class discussions.

I want to feel a struggle with (or for) ideas.
I like to see the inherent contradictions discussed (the importance of the community over self, yet self is talked about in most of the literature we read—though the term "literature" has been debated).

I want to hear your voice saying not what it thinks it should say, but what it wants to say.
I want to hear a creation myth for your voice using a different way of thinking than you have before.
I want to see you leading, not me thinking (or coming up with), Where is it you're going?

I expect you to carry through with the expectations you set up.

I want you to say, this is where we are going, and then take the reader there.
I don't want to be let down.

I want you to write until you find it hard to trust yourself.

Freedom is harder than receiving direct directions.
I want you to face your paper with respect. I want you to act like it is bigger than you.
I want to see you rise to meet it.

That is all.

As we are running out of time to get through *Native American Literature: An Anthology,* I give them excerpts as we get into book reports from our reading list:

These passages are from "The Man Made of Words," by N. Scott Momaday, *Native American Literature: An Anthology,* chapter 8 (which reminds me of the surreal *cocoon* scene in "Black Eagle Child" where Young Bear pastes words to himself).

It seems to me that in a certain sense we are all made of words, and that our most essential being consists in language. It is the element in which we think and dream and act, in which we live our daily lives (636).

We are what we imagine. Our very existence consists in our imagination of ourselves. Our best destiny is at least to imagine completely who and what and *that* we are. The greatest tragedy that can befall us is to go unimagined (641).

Man has consummate being in language, and there only. The state of human *being* is an idea, an idea that man has of himself. Only when he is embodied in an idea, and the idea is realized in language, can man take possession of himself. In our particular frame of reference, this is to say that man achieves the fullest realization of his humanity in such an art and product of the imagination as literature—and here I use the term "literature" in its broadest sense (642).

(Another definition of "literature"—after reading Momaday: an imaginative experience realized in language that is revealed over time and has many meanings.) ("I have lived with the story of the arrowmaker for many years," Momaday says, "and I am sure that I do not yet understand it in all of its consequent meanings" [635].) The story: A Kiowa was making an arrow, he knew someone was outside the door his teepee, he said (in Kiowa) if you understand my words, you will make yourself known. The spy did not, and the arrowmaker shot him with the arrow [653].

Do you see what happens when the imagination is superimposed upon a historical event? It becomes a story. (This is said after describing the 1833 meteor shower: "With the coming of dawn, there began a new and darker age for the Kiowa—Within four years of the falling stars the Kiowas signed their first treaty with the government; within twenty, four major epidemics of smallpox and cholera destroyed more than half their number; and within scarcely more than a generation their horses were taken from them and the herds of buffalo were slaughtered and left to waste on the plains—They could say to themselves, "Yes, it was all meant to be in its turn. The order of the world was broken, it was clear. Even the stars were shaken loose in the night sky" (642–43). The imagination of meaning was not much, perhaps, but it was all they had, and it was enough to sustain them.

Some of the books on the reading list:

Black Elk Speaks, *John Neihardt*
House Made of Dawn, *N. Scott Momaday*
Ceremony, *Leslie Silko*
Winter in the Blood, *James Welch*
Love Medicine, *Louise Erdrich*
Tales from the Glittering World, *Irvin Morris*
Shadow Distance: A Reader, *Gerald Vizenor*
Ohitika Woman, *Mary Brave Bird*
Tonto and the Lone Ranger Fist Fight in Heaven, *Sherman Alexie*

I spend the whole day reading papers for my Native American literature class. I finish reading the anthology. The grades: A (3), A– (6), B+ (5). I think one B+ should have been a B. Maybe two. Then I would have made one A– a B+. Grading is arbitrary. A judgment call. Subject to pressure for A's. Maybe I should have shifted them all down one place.

I look through Scott Momaday's *House Made of Dawn* because I am near the place it was written.

In the evening, I work on one of the novels I brought with me.

"Once in his life a man ought to concentrate his mind upon the remembered earth, I believe. He ought to give himself up to a particular landscape in his experience, to look at it from as many angles as he can, to wonder about, to dwell upon it" (*The Man Made of Words,* by N. Scott Momaday).

I remember many landscapes when I was growing up. Places in the woods; a copse of trees where I would go.

When my father was transferred to the Armour plant in Indianapolis, we made a trip to one of the state parks, Turkey Run, possibly. We were with neighbors. I don't know what happened. But there was a connection to the land, to the trees, to the leaves, whatever was there. Something connected directly to my sense of being. It was an act of recognition, an act of *being* I still carry. It was the first time I remembered hearing the land.

I pass back the papers in Native American literature. I feel there is dissatisfaction over the remarks I made. I feel my headache come back. Grading also is an emotional burden. I don't like the power students have to influence the grades they are given.

Once again, I spend the morning reading, writing. After the afternoon fiction workshop, I go to Harry's Road House just north of Santa Fe for dinner with other faculty.

At dinner, someone tells me a story about the spirit woman, *La Llorona,* in the River House. I ask the others about her. *Yes, she's there,* they say. *You can hear her wailing at night.*

I drive back to NAPS under a brilliant moon. It is so bright there are no stars. Because I am in a place I don't particularly want to be, I think of the transparency of travel, the things that pass through. I was on I-65 in Indiana after a reading in Chicago on my roundabout way to New Mexico when a car turned left illegally on a *crossover*. I saw the sudden stop of cars ahead of me. It was dark; I could not stop fast enough. The car ahead of me was rushing toward me, I jerked the wheel to the right; somehow no car was in the other lane. I think of the change in landscape as I travel. The topography of movement. The portability. The momentum of travel. Again, it is my ancestors I hear saying, *go*. When I leave August sixth, I will drive north on I-25 through Colorado, east across Nebraska and Iowa on I-80, and north on I-35 at Des Moines to Minnesota.

I'm sitting in bed reading about 11:00 when I hear the voices. Only I think they are coyotes. Eerie, barking, cawing, cackling voices, somewhere in the valley. I turn the light off. I'm tired anyway. I still hear the coyotes. I hear the wind in the piñons and junipers outside the deck. The roof is shaking with wind.

There, in all the noises, I hear the wailing of *La Llorona*. I don't feel fear. Maybe I should.

"Did you hear anything last night?" They ask at lunch.

"Yes, I did, but I think it was coyotes," I say. "I haven't heard the coyotes the whole time I've been here. But after you tell me about *La Llorona*, I hear her voice. It's like in the New Testament: You sin if you think it's a sin. If you're aware it's a sin. Otherwise you're fine. You seem to know whatever your eyes have been opened to."

They tell me it's more than a spirit woman. "There're other spirits down by the Pecos. The wind carries them, the piñons."

"But there's nothing in the house any spirit would care about," I say.

"Maybe before the house was here."

It's true. I remember a house in Oklahoma that I later thought was on land where something had happened. I could feel it sometimes.

"I don't think they like the River House," I say. "I think they're trying to push it down the hill. Except then it would clog the river. Maybe it's just the erosion."

"Nature helps the spirits," someone says.

"But I don't feel afraid, not yet anyway."

"They're good spirits. They're discerning. You aren't mean."

I hear knocking in the house again in the afternoon. It seems funny this time.

We have a discussion about the Trickster in Native American literature. It is anything with the attribute of duality. Anything that steps outside boundaries. Christianity. Alcohol. Depending on which way you take it. What a precarious balance survival is. As William Heyen said of poetry, it opens up the possibilities, so the concept of the Trickster opens up levels in the ways of thinking about things.

While reading papers, I return to my reading in the book of Job. I hear the voice of one daughter in particular: She is left without a name along with two sisters and seven brothers. She was in a house when a wind came and blew the house down upon them and killed them all.

Later other sons and daughters were born to Job and his wife. Did they ever think of their first children?

What could the daughter of Job have said? Was she was gone before she had a chance to think, and what did she think? Had she married? Had she had children? They all were eating and drinking in the brother's house. They chose to be together. Did she do anything besides eat and drink in her brother's house, suddenly gone as if she wasn't there? Did she question God when she stood before him? Was she a rebel? A rich man's spoiled daughter, angry that she couldn't go on eating and drinking?

The architecture of history is a past of tactical spaces. It is new historical thinking. The left-out voices let in. It is American strategies. Language as land, as place, as geography.

I come from a history of stockyards: railroad tracks, old brick warehouses, wood floors, meat carts with their metal wheels making grooves. The cattle divided according to modernism, part by part; the hunt industrialized. The hunt retooled. Reweaponed. The old cattle cars. Standing still, they moved. Now, in postmodernism, hoof is joined to tail, ear to leg.

I've wanted to write in the voice of an animal (especially a pig caged in a hog barn): *On a bright morning taken from the pen; the room at the top of the ramp; the sudden knife cutting the throat that could have made sound. The hooks and chains. Maybe without thought walking in line, the smell, what was it?—a sudden burst of fear, pain—then nothing?*

This is my father (of the sparkling Fourth) over the confluence of the Kaw and Missouri Rivers. Yes, they knew they would die, my father said, but it was quick, mercifully quick. Soundless at least, because their vocal cords were cut. Maybe it's why the kill was on the second floor: for the ascent heavenward.

Imagine this place in July.

"Unified Front," Antonya Nelson,
Best American Short Stories, 1998

I HAVE TWO days of classes left: Native American literature on Monday, fiction on Tuesday. Then graduation is on Thursday. After I gave a reading the first week I was at Bread Loaf, the seniors asked me to give the final address at graduation.

In the fiction class, students want a definition of a short story: It tells us a little of what we know a lot about. "People in realistic, detailed situations," Ray Carver (I think) once said. "But the situations aren't always realistic," a student said. "A short story is about someone who is going through an experience from which they will learn something," I say. Someone else doesn't buy that. "A short story is something in which the reader discovers another layer of reality under the one on the page. A story is a little medicine bundle of magic. A grandmother's quilt that carries stories of the pieces of materials she used."

What is the history of the short story? I suppose the first story was four words: "Let there be light." The books of the Old Testament including Job, Ruth, and Jonah are some of the oldest stories in our Western culture. *The Canterbury Tales,* the *Decameron* are others. In America, Washington Irving wrote his *Sketch Book.* Others followed, developing the structure that became the short story: A character who wants something, but something gets in the way. There is conflict/resolution, character change, development, and some sort of epiphany.

A short story is something you need a potholder for. (July is thirty-one potholders sewn together like a quilt.) A story is also a potholder to hold against the world.

What do I want the class to get? A quilt-like effect. A splaying of meaning. Just as poetry comes from somewhere between the upper and lower mind. So does fiction. There is plot, action, character, theme. What it transcends to is an experience of reading and understanding that opens up possibilities.

This magic box of possibility. This calendar of events. This summation of something beyond the parts.

In our anthology is Meg Wolitzer's "Tea at the House," in which a young woman grows up in a hospital for the insane because her father is the director. He has people come to his house for tea (those on the verge of release). One of the young men wakens the character to her first sexual experience. There is a line early on: *Electricity in Use.* She wonders what that means. Of course, she will soon experience electricity of another kind. The sensual awakening. A jolt of an experience. Later, he sends a letter to her father. He reads it; she sees the red seal (it is written on Harvard stationery). To me, it is a symbol of the hymen she lost with the young man. The red spot she found with him. The electricity of recognition of symbol, of portent, of the layers a story should have.

In the end, I'm not sure—maybe it was a seal between the men to ignore the daughter; a gentlemen's agreement. They will have theirs. It is sealed.

How much relies on interpretation?

The other class has needed a potholder.

I remember thinking what I wanted for the summer in Native American literature, and I decided to go through a new anthology because it provided a quilt of voices, tessellate as Native American literature with its gathering of many voices trying (1) to remember, (2) to protest, (3) to envision a future, (4) to make sense of tradition, of acculturation, of combinations of both, of walking in two worlds, maybe several worlds.

I wanted a book that would give the idea of the multiplicity available in a culture which is a pattern of many cultures within the same race. And I wanted to know what the students made of them. (How they pieced together a quilt of understanding.) I wanted to know what I would do with them.

I wanted to hear as many voices as possible. It is a different way to enter a course. It's the hard way.

But what do you think otherness is? What do you think Native American literature is? It can be an experience of uncertainty and frustration. You make whatever answers there are for yourself. An act of fiction, a placement of geography onto dialogue, a place made of words.

There are different ways to realize the world. You can't walk in and assume you know what another culture is like. Or appropriate that culture as yours. It can't be given to you the way you want it.

For me, to have some of the Indian blood but not to be in the world that blood is from is to know what you don't want to know. That a culture existed and still exists here in the margins of our nation that I would be better off knowing. It is the sense of loss and erasure through acculturation.

I am in trouble on the last day of Native American literature. I know they have been dissatisfied with the class. I ask for criticism. *I didn't say enough. I didn't give enough. Critical theory was missing. My voice was absent. There was no structure. They teach all year. They didn't want to take an active part. The reading materials were depressing.*

One particularly angry young man said he was just going to read his course evaluation for his final project. I had failed as a teacher, but he was feeling less angry at the moment. So he didn't read it. But for his final project he had nothing in particular to say, other than his anger. Maybe he was on the way to an understanding of Native American literature, though I didn't intend it that way.

I finish my fiction class the next day, on August third. It was a class that went well. I pack and give the commencement address August fifth. Afterwards, there is a dinner and a mariachi band.

The next morning, August sixth, I leave before dawn for the two-day drive back to Minnesota, dismissed, relegated back to *flyover* land. I will have driven just over six thousand miles since I left on June seventeenth on a roundabout trip that went from St. Paul to Chicago to Atlanta to Rowe, New Mexico, my file boxes buckled into the backseat as if passengers. A file box buckled into the front seat also, a pillow against the window as if someone were sleeping there.

I place my philosophy of driving on the road: just keep going toward the destination, no matter how far ahead. St. Paul to Chicago. Then the hundred-mile jaunts: Indianapolis to Cincinnati (the same hundred miles I used to drive from Tulsa to Oklahoma City when I lived in Oklahoma), Cincinnati to Lexington to Knoxville to Chattanooga to Atlanta, and you find yourself across the country.

I love gasoline, its oily colors. Down one hill and up another past the trucks, which are the regulators of the road. When oncoming traffic backed up for miles, I saw trucks in the inside lane stop cars from getting ahead of cars already in line. I hate to pass animal-transport trucks, most of them carrying shoats. They did not step willingly into the truck.

Now I travel north on I-25 from New Mexico through Colorado, east across Nebraska and Iowa on I-80, and north on I-35 at Des Moines to Minnesota.

In St. Paul, I unpack the car and drive to the Blue Mounds Reading series in Luverne, Minnesota, the next weekend.

After the reading in Luverne, I decide to drive the 250 miles back to St. Paul instead of spending the night. I drive east on I-90 in the dark. Bikers pass from their summer *blowout* (fallout) in Sturgis, South Dakota, headed back east to Wisconsin or Michigan, or wherever they're from, their headbands blowing in the wind, their red taillights sparking the dark night. The fury of their engines ripples the highway. They are black, flying hot pads. Overhead, the white sparks of the Perseid meteor shower.

TRANSMOTION

. . . that sense of Native motion

I am a bird who rises from the earth, and flies far up, into the skies, out of human sight; but though not visible to the eye, my voice is heard from afar, and resounds over the earth.

> Keeshkumun
> from *Fugitive Poses,* Gerald Vizenor

—and his dress filled the temple.
> Isaiah 6:1

THE HOLY HAS always seemed unholy to me. Or at least ordinary in the central Great Plains of America where I've lived. In Protestant, Holy Ghost country. A hidden place. A place as though it weren't there. A place streaked with the vapor trails of passing planes.

My father worked for Armour, coming north from the Arkansas/Oklahoma border to Kansas City for work during the Depression. He was transferred to Armour stockyards in the Midwest, then from Indianapolis to Denver, from Kansas City to Iowa. All the time we went to church.

Because of church we survived the roads we passed in blizzards. The moving van somewhere behind us with my chest of drawers like a suitcase, going here to there; my mattress turned up on edge, let down again in one bedroom before sailing to another. It was when the packing plants were huge wooden ships that began to leak. Slowly they were razed. My father was part of that process. His life closed down along with the plants, and he is in the grave where he sent all those cattle.

We attended church every Sunday morning. When we moved, a new church was chosen like a sturdy winter coat. Sunday mornings happened only in church. Nothing else went on anywhere.

Once, in a flash of lightning, a light pole split behind our house. Its blue light filled the room / was the closest I can tell you to what it would be like to be struck with the Holy Ghost. The power you need to get through the weather on the Great Plains. The extremes of heat and cold. The entry into new classrooms

and Sunday schools. Everyone stared. The sun stared. The stars stared. The Holy
Ghost flew in a blue dress with all His spirits. Like toast and the crumbs. When
I found a chair, everyone's heads turned back to the front of the room. The Holy
Ghost held them there.

I have been born again by Jesus' blood. Filled with the Holy Ghost. I can't
say which I like better. They are children asking whom you love most. But you say
you are BOTH my favorites. I speak in tongues. I tell them in tongues. They are
both the best. And God up there over them somewhere is the best also, like the
three brothers who lived behind me and overshadowed my house.

God, the Word, and the Spirit, which is the spoken voice of the Word. The
mystery wrapped in the Trinity.

Now my parents are in their graves side by side in Kansas City, as if asleep
in their twin beds. I am in Minnesota, traveling back now and then. I am in my own
life when I thought I would no longer be moving with my furniture, house to house,
but I kept moving when I had decided to settle FOREVER in one place. But the
road kept calling and I shifted across the Great Plains states. My sense of place is
in the moving.

You may not understand. Not being from here. How it is when the Holy
Ghost enters your life like a brother-in-law you know is going to be there a while.
He may not leave and intrudes/invades your house like the Foreign Legion. You
have NOTHING left He doesn't own. He asks for a potato and you give it to Him.
You feel a pilot helmet on your head / you say you don't fly but you ascend to the
clouds / to the Northern Lights / your duck's feet lifted back like paddles of a boat
when the duck flies.

You move so often, sometimes you cannot stop. You feel your mother's
ancestors still in boats crossing the Atlantic from Germany and England. Your
father's people still walking to Oklahoma on the forced migration of the Cherokee.
When you are grown, you still make your own migrations from Oklahoma to Iowa
to Minnesota.

You're in a Pentecostal church on the Great Plains / the Holy Spirit flies
low in His blue dress. Yo. A Moving Van. Carrying all you have packed inside. I
have broken clothes He mends. I have sheep He crates for moving. Sometimes I
cannot see my way. I have a duck's foot for a hand. What are you doing a sloppy,
ragged job like that for? / I ask myself. But He drives all over the place. He and the

friends. Those blue-dress flyers, buzzing. Smearing the windshield they kiss. They leave a fog with their paraffin lips.

In a ceremony He gets a new name: The-Holy-Ghost-Who-Hangs-in-the-Blue-Folds-of-Air-Above-the-Road-Which-the-Great-Plains-Is. The scriptures are the well-holes of the ear. The oil-pools of the eye. The Holy Ghost gives you a topography map. He lifts you above the plains with the skywriting He does. Sometimes you see the little blue moons circling.

The car with the water bag hanging from the hood ornament in case there's a few miles between gas stations. You wouldn't remember the days when gas was far apart. *You stop here; there won't be another for 249 miles.*

Give me these deep waters I do not have a dipper for, that do not come easily. Give me well water. Magic water. Firewater of the Spirit. The water turned inside out. The water of the Word that opens up Possibilities. I speak-into-being the road ahead. Not magically making the world I want, but lining up what the Holy Ghost wants. The rain that falls after lightning pokes its finger from the sky.

There are many wells in the Great Plains.

The Bible itself is a well.

For years I drove the back roads of Oklahoma. The Spirits slid by the car. I could never outrun them. If I'd had a gun, I could not stop them. They wore old ghost dance shirts with hands printed on their chests. They wore the blue dresses. I've already said that.

The woman at the well (John 4) asked where she should worship: in the mountains or in Jerusalem. *It doesn't matter,* the Word said. The Father seeks those who worship him in spirit and in truth. This is the landscape where it is done.

The Holy Ghost slashes Difficulties like tires. He blasts them. The Holy Ghost is the nozzle I see like a funnel. I hear it clank against the tank. I hear the hiss of the cap loosened on a hot day. I smell the gas going into my tank.

I've been outnumbered. I have been where there was no way out. Yet I drove across Oklahoma to Minnesota on the Word that said I could. The motor-cycles passed / they surrounded, but the Holy Spirit sent his covered dish. Often it is in that hard place where the Spirits wait. Sometimes Jesus pushes them out of the way / waving now as I pass.

Sometimes I see the Holy Ghost dangling in His place.

Lord of Transformation.
Lord of the Road.
Lord of Potholders.
Lord of the Cattle.
Lord of Buffalo.
Lord of the Far Horizon.
Lord of the Roily Sea.
Lord of Wind.
Lord of Cloud.
Lord of Northern Lights.
Lord of Cold.
Lord of Tongues.
Lord of the Ear Drum.
Lord of the Prairie.
Lord of the Tornado.
Lord of the Rock.
Lord of the Oasis.
Lord of the Flood Gate.
Lord of the Plateau.
Lord of the Fox.
Lord of the Fish Net.
Lord of Transmotion.
Lord of the Well.

INDIAN GUIDE

If one were only an Indian, instantly alert, and on a running horse, leaning into the wind, kept on quivering jerkily over the quivering ground, until one shed one's spurs, for there needed no spurs, threw away the reins, for there needed no reins, and hardly saw that the land before one was smoothly shorn heath when horse's neck and head would be already gone.

> FRANZ KAFKA, *The Wish to Be a Red Indian*,
> translated by Willa and Edwin Muir

All things are in the process and nothing stays still.
All things are in motion all the time.

> HERACLITUS, 500 B.C.

190,000 acres of land had been surface mined of coal by the mid-20th century.

Strip mining necessarily overhauls the landscape.

> ENCYCLOPEDIA BRITANNICA

Landscape is a story. It carries what passes there, what happened there, rather. The land is an Indian guide.

Section One

My maternal grandfather (the European side of the family) had a farm in Bourbon County, Kansas, along the Missouri border. When I was a girl, we drove there from Kansas City, where my father worked in the stockyards.

My grandfather's first farm, which had belonged to his father, was near Hume, Missouri, Howard Township, Bates County, resting against the Kansas border. In 1934, Sinclair Coal Company bought the land for strip mining, and my grandfather moved from Missouri to Kansas to farm just a few miles from the state line.

In the years that followed, the mining company left mounds of mined land in Missouri where my grandfather and his father had farmed. I remember the enormous gray beehives of barren land.

Section Two

(From *Mineral Wealth of Missouri*, two lectures delivered by Professor C. D. Wilber, inspector of mining lands, in the Hall of Representatives in Jefferson City, Missouri, February 17 and 18, 1870; with gratefulness to *Divine Beneficence* for placing coal near the surface, and with epic allusions to Cicero, Demosthenes, Horace, Virgil, Ovid, Aladdin's Lamp, the novels of Dickens and Thackeray, and Abraham, Isaac, and Jacob).

> *Coal is universally but not evenly distributed though this area. These coal beds lie so near the surface as to admit of stripping. A majority of farmers have a coal mine at home. When the coal bed is scant, a journey of several inches is sometimes performed. And when stripping requires too much labor, the next farm may offer a better opening.*
>
> *Let us delve and mine, measure and analyze, and run to and fro on the land until we have greatly increased knowledge and made it available to men of skill and industry.*

Barns, sheds, houses bulldozed—fields upturned, leaving the earth raw and scraped. Did Professor Wilber ever look back to see what skill and industry left? Did anyone consider the devastation of the land?

What must the huge electric shovel have sounded like? What kind of fear shook the burrows of the small animals as the mouth of the land was pried open, the teeth pulled out, the mouth never closed again?

Does the bluestem call from under the earth? The black-eyed Susan, tickseed, wild columbine, yarrow, sunflower, morning glory, prairie clover, aster, leadplant, Queen Anne's lace? What about the fields? The deer, antelope, elk, buffalo, quail, pheasant, wild turkey?

Gone to make iron in furnaces, steam in factories, mills, locomotives, and gasworks, and heating in buildings and houses.

Could the deer, the clover, stand up to that?

Years after the mining company left, the mounds of upturned land are still swollen with rage.

Section Three

In October 1999, sixty-five years after the Sinclair Coal Company pushed my
grandfather off his farm near Hume, Missouri, I drove sixty-nine miles south from
Kansas City on Kansas Highway 69 to see the strip mines I remembered.

I passed Bucyrus and Louisburg, where the highway narrows from double
to a single lane. I passed the old Civil War battlefield at Trading Post. I passed the
marshy edge of the Marias des Cygnes wildlife reserve, where as a child on the
way to my grandfather's farm, we went off the road in an ice storm, and my father
walked to the nearest farm, and a farmer came and pulled us out of the ditch on the
northbound shoulder, and we turned around and headed south again.

At a place of road construction, I was stopped behind a long line of cars
and trucks while oncoming traffic passed. I tried to roll the windows down, but
the wind and dust were too strong. I had to keep all windows closed but for the
driver's side. I listened to the land as I looked into the field across the highway.
The autumn was dry. The wind bent the thickets and weeds beside the road. The
wide farm country sallowed under the sun. The wind hissed.

A flagman held our impatience steady until the northbound traffic passed.
Then the little truck with its orange flag led the southbound traffic into the oncoming lane, around the construction, while other northbound traffic gathered ahead,
stopped by another flagman farther down the road than we could yet see.

At Prescott, Kansas, I turned east on State Road 239. It was five miles to
Missouri. Just across the border—there were the mounds of mined land, now
covered with short trees, thickets, and prairie grass—separated by moats of water.
State Road 239, which had been straight for its five miles in Kansas, began curving
between the mounds at sharp angles. Signs were posted: *25 miles an hour. 5 miles an
hour.*

I passed another sign: *140 acres for sale.*

There were a few plowed fields wedged between the mounds of mined land,
probably less than an acre each.

Then I was in Hume. Its town square vacant. The few people looking as I
passed. Post office. Old gas station. Boarded-up storefronts around the square.
In one of them, Great Uncle John had made shoes. A street sign: *Railroad* (though

none was there). Down a dirt road off the square, the one brick school, grades K–12, across the street from the house that had been Uncle John and Aunt Maud's. Then the church where my grandfather's and grandmother's funeral services were held.

I took several county roads from Hume. The wind lifted dust into the air behind the car. The land was covered with the old humps of land. Maybe they could be the ghost of Osage villages. Or the mound builders. Or other tribes that had passed. (Missouri and Kansas [Canzes] were names of Indian tribes. Kansas also is supposed to mean *blue smoke*, because of all the prairie fires. Does that mean the name of the Canzes Indians also meant *blue smoke?* Or had the name been subverted somehow? Or had more than one meaning? Language itself undergoes the same disruption as the land.)

There's a natural formation a mile south of Hume called *Rocky Mound*. Originally the land was occupied by the Osage, who used the mound as a lookout. According to historical records, the French explorer De Tissent visited the mounds in 1719. In 1806, Zebulon Pike recorded a visit. In 1821, when Missouri became a state, the French fur trader Papin recorded his visit. The treaty of 1837 moved the Osage farther west. By 1850, settlers began occupying the government lands. By 1880, a *Survey Plat of Town of Howard* recorded Railroad Street, Main Street, Osage Alley, Hume Street. But the name Howard was changed to Hume because of Howard's Mill nearby.

I looked for Rocky Mound to the south, and the old farm somewhere a mile west of Hume. The farmhouse, of course, wouldn't have been there, but the land, of course, would be. I drove down several more roads but couldn't recognize any place. The old farm was gone before I was born. Maybe I was hoping for an instinct, for the land as an Indian guide, but there was none.

In the cemetery near Hume, I stood at my grandparents' grave: Forest and Anna Myrtle Wood. Next to them were H. K. and Frances Wood, my maternal great-grandparents. Others were there: John and Maud Adams, Aubrey; my grandfather's brother, who died as a baby in 1882; and Ruth Wood, my grandmother's first child, who was stillborn in 1908.

They were people who lived and died to themselves. The last thing they wanted to do was to stand out. They measured their affection with a teaspoon. I remember the heavy gravy, the grease, the chicken my grandmother had beheaded. Dinner at my maternal grandparents' farmhouse was something like the aftermath on a battlefield. I had the feeling something intense was over, though it lingered in the air. The meals were sturdy. Hardy. I was not wanted. I was in the way. What was wrong with me? It was a tough life on the farm. There was no patience, tolerance, respect for anything but hard work. And there was silence about the truth that was behind the silence.

I remembered the windy Missouri/Kansas prairie from my childhood. The corner of the head scarf battering my head. I still have photos, the end of my scarf pointing straight out, sometimes blurred because of the flapping. My round face squatty, wide-nosed, with an overall ugliness or plainness. I would be able to pass through the world unnoticed.

Section Four

In some way, this is about the moon (strip mining leaves a moon surface on the land it strips); the full moon rising like a silo cap when it sits, half-up, on the land. Then the moon is full and round in the sky, as if all the restless headlights on the road had been rounded up in a corral.

Does not the moon look trampled?

Or maybe more like a scorched potholder?

The moon grows smaller as it climbs. Soon it is a lightbulb down a dark corridor through the hallway of trees, flickering on scattered ponds and rivers, the metal roofs of barns and sheds.

I remember the dark winding road we used to take to Arkansas to visit my father's family, though we didn't drive there after dark. (His family was his Cherokee mother with a row of corn and a few pigs.) I remember waiting for the ferry that would take us across Norfolk Lake to my paternal grandmother's farm. I remember the cars coming up the hill from the landing. Then it was our turn to drive down the hill and on to the ferry.

Missouri, Kansas, Oklahoma, Arkansas: my four-cornered world.

The dried cornstalks were huge praying mantises; the autumn trees painted like a Mexican border town (though I'd never been to Mexico).

Mine is not a verb but a noun. It is a thing. An object. Static. Dead. Not moving. There to stay. Not only coal, but iron, lead, zinc, tin, and copper, taken from the land south in Missouri from Hume to Joplin.

A register of a few of the mines: Minor Heir, Ice Plant, Black Cat, Rampage, Pawnee, Twin Cities, Grasshopper, Ten O'Clock, Mt. Ararat, Gussier, Shoestring, What Cheer, Reliance, Trinity, Good Friday, Little Mary, Seven Devils, Seven Angels, Horseshoe, Florence, Beulah, Grace, Pocohontas, Hercules, Providence, Battle Ax, Katydid, Gray Goose, Vinegar Hill, White Dog, Red Dog, Water Dog, Bull Dog, Orphan Boy, Big Hit, Comet, Stump, Hoo-Hoo, Plymouth Rock.

Section Five

Shake the coal out of its bed. Shiver off the soil.

(Hiss on the history of strip mining.)

Section Six

An Osage story of land transformation:

Rocky Mound is a vehicle the Maker could drive away, but somehow the wheels never arrive.

An electric shovel married the land; the barren mounds are their children.

The Maker undressed, leaving his garments on the floor, turned inside out, with seams, pockets, lining, the wrong side showing.

The mounds of strip mines are the remains of a battlefield where old spirits tried to step to the sky from the underworld but were turned back.

Section Seven

Encyclopedia Britannica: "Coal is a black storehouse of the sun." It is fossilized plant material, preserved by burial, full of carbon the plants abstracted from the air.

Professor Wilber: *"The coal fields of Missouri are ample."*

Tons and tons of it were ripped from the land, leaving the ravaged landscape a ward of the state, now listening to the plea for legislation for land reclamation.

What do we have but a synecdoche, a part for the whole? (Because the whole is too frightening—as if unity were unbearable.)

But what is memory but something dislodged?

More often it is a metonymy, not even a part connected with the whole, but an abstract, somehow loosely, indirectly identified with. (The memory of the strip mines; the heat that comes when I think of what strip mining did to the land; the writing about it as a potholder to hold the memory.)

The whole itself stuck with a perspective depending upon which viewpoint it is viewed from, and from what place and time.

"160 acres underlaid with coal."

Strip mining fueled the industry of America but ruined the land from which the coal was taken.

There were fragments of an old landscape (of what is not seen) on my trip. Images of the sun glinting off thin strips of water in the strip pits like Civil War soldiers with a piece of mirror reflecting the sun. There were flashbacks to the turmoil my mother expressed on her deathbed. She would say, *"Father, let me in"*; her voice, fretful, panicked at times. During her life, she didn't talk about her feelings. We never talked about what mattered. But in the last few days before her death, she talked nonstop about her life. It wasn't conversation but a rerun of memories when she was out of her head, or maybe I should say in her head.

It was a surreal landscape: a farmhouse, a coal bucket at the back door, the shiny black pieces of coal like the moon reflecting off a pond at night. A green metal magazine. (Where did it come from?) Somehow a memory of something warped into the shape it bears (though might not actually have had).

The land humped with mounds.

Memory upturns the past, leaving *chaptered mounds.* It fills the present with wavering images, as if seen through old, lead-window-glass. I wasn't sent to an orphanage. Maybe I was kept like an article they thought they would need later. Or it was against the law to get rid of. Yet there was something in that coldness that drew me on. The pattern of sun on the bed. A sense of something better ahead.

(Unfolding a map is easy. It's folding it back together that's hard.)

Professor Wilber, speaking of a coal vein (though it could have been memory): *"It is probably the head of the king bolt, binding two hemispheres together."*

There was a house in Oklahoma we lived in once. I felt something when I first walked in the door: a quickening, a realization. But I misread it as, *"This is my house,"* when what it meant was, *"This house is on land that belongs to something that happened."*

If I had to say what I felt happened on the land, I would say the words, *Indian or settler, maybe both, an encampment under the hot, white sun, a death and burial.*

I felt an *otherness* while I lived in that house in Oklahoma.

If I had to say further, I would say I felt a *grieving* because of what happened there. It's a word for an image mined from the memory of a feeling I had in the house I lived in once.

I'm not sure I felt all of it while I lived there, but it came as a gradual awareness, most of it after I moved.

That's probably what happened there.

Section Eight

The continuation of mining and strip mining is a migration across the land. Mountaintop mining has been in the news lately, blasting the tops off mountains to get at the coal, letting the rubble fall into the valleys. As long as there is anything left to take, human *industry* will take it.

But what of extinction? (which is always with us): The Indian tribes. The land. Species of birds and animals. What does it matter if the fields were pushed off the beds of coal and the coal removed from the land and the land left in heaps like an unmade bed? Consumerism is astounding. As is the knowledge that nothing will stop it.

But aren't we doing to nature what nature does to itself? Volcano, earthquake, hurricane, tidal wave change and reshape the earth. Countless insects and animals prey upon one another. Upheaval and destruction are with us at every turn.

In *Pilgrim at Tinker Creek,* Annie Dillard writes about the cruelty she finds in nature. She questions what kind of world we live in. She says the robin "may die the most gruesome of slow deaths, and nature is no less pleased." Dillard goes on to ask if we are moral creatures in an amoral world.

If landscape is a story, it is a story I read myself into. It is a story, therefore, of myself. What if it is an inner landscape made visible?

Nature is full of grandeur and brutality, as Dillard observes. But aren't those dichotomies observable also in human nature, which has produced Hitler and St. Francis?

Don't I feel those polarities in myself also (though not as extreme)? Chug up the earth. Take it for myself. Other times, I live with a conscience for others. More often, I vacillate between the two. The same human nature in me is capable of both selfishness and selflessness. I am a mixed bag. Like nature.

The Apostle Paul came to that same realization in the New Testament Book of Romans, chapter 7. *"For the good that I would, I do not; but the evil which I would not, that I do"* (7:19). *"I see another law in my members, warring against the law of my mind"* (7:23). *"Who can deliver me from the body of this death?"* (7:24).

Maybe instead of morality versus amorality, it is a question of multi-morality in a multi-moral world. I'm not sure what that means. I'm not sure I like what it could mean. I need to believe in good and evil. I need the separation. The security of it.

I also know this is the earth of sameness and change, mostly change.

The day of the October trip to the strip mines was clear and dusty; the sun a hot plate bearing down on the air. The dried leaves and brush spoke as I walked through them. They asked for rain. The birds cawed and twittered. There was a heavy settledness in the brittle, weedy wildlife sanctuary of the strip mines. There was a stillness after the enormous upheaval, the madness of bedlam, the scars left by rapers, pillagers. The coal they took now long used up, and school had just let out. The yellow buses traveled down the road past the cemetery where Aubrey, the baby, slept, who had never seen school nor mined land nor done much of anything, though the mining must have shaken his grave. It was one of those high afternoons on the dusty throne of the earth.

A part of a greater force and mystery still unknown.

Section Nine

If landscape is a story I read myself into, I also read others into it. When I passed the Hume school on my trip, I remember a boy my mother had told me about. He had broken his ankle in the schoolyard. It never healed the way it should. He limped and had pain all his life. Then my mother read in the local newspaper that he had had his foot amputated. He must have been in his sixties by then. I think I heard his cries when I passed the schoolyard. Not with my ears, but somewhere; the land stores the noises of what happened there. Maybe I also heard a room in some farmhouse, the bloody quilt, the cries from a boy whose ankle would never heal.

If landscape is an Indian guide, it is a wooden Indian. A fiction made from fiction. Heaped with what it is not: gray, gutted piles of land as though they were the way the land was supposed to be.

Acres and acres of mined land, itself nearly as real as a real landscape. A clumpy agreement with industry for garishness and unnaturalness.

But it was my own fields, shoveled up, I saw in the land. To get to the coal underneath. To take from one place to use in another. What was left was my own mined land that resonated with the strip mines I saw. A part indirectly related to the whole of a life torn up.

A recognition of land as self and self as land. A seeing of the other in terms of itself.

Section Ten

That night I returned from the strip mines, the quarter moon was a letter *C. C the land under the sky. C the C of darkness.*

HOG BARN

Does not wisdom cry?
    —PROVERBS 8:1

I SMELL THE hog barns in Iowa as I return to Minnesota. I have wanted to write about them from the hog's perspective. But how to do it?

I begin to collect what is said about the hog, pig, swine, porker, hogget, hoggy, shoat, boar, sow, razorback, peccary.

An animal lives as a machine lives.
    —DESCARTES

Animalium hoc maxime brutum, animamque ei pro sale datam non inlepide existsimabatur. (The pig is the most brutish of animals, and there used to be a not unattractive idea that its soul was given it to serve as salt.)
    —CICERO QUOTING CHRYSIPPUS

It is a known fact that some pigs carried off by pirates, crowded to one side of the ship until it capsized and sank, and they swam back to shore.
    Moreover, a pig can lead a herd to the market place and find its way back home; and wild hogs know how to obliterate their tracks by crossing marshy ground.
    —PLINY, *Natural History,* Libri VIII, LXXVII

You can't say the word pig on a boat because a pig can't swim, or if they try, they slit their throats with their hooves.
    —LINDA GREENWALD, *The Hungry Ocean,* Fresh Air, NPR

A pig is turned into bacon, bacon becomes food that gives unity and purpose to the imagination.

Edward, seeing the earliest blue line of things to come, finished his whiskey. Then he went to the icebox for the bacon, which will always be with us.

　　　—WILLIAM KENNEDY, *The Flaming Corsage*

I even find animals, if not necessarily pigs, in the Book of Revelation:

And I heard the voice of many angels around the throne and the BEASTS and the elders: and the number of them was ten thousand times ten thousand.

　　　—REVELATION 5:11

BEASTS around the throne!?

And EVERY CREATURE that is in heaven, and on the earth, and under the earth, and such as are in the seas, and all that are in them, I heard saying, Blessing, and honor, and glory, and power unto him that sits upon the throne, and unto the Lamb forever and ever.

　　　—REVELATION 5:13

Even Solomon, in his wisdom, spoke of the BEASTS in I Kings 4:33.
But how would the pig speak for itself?
We know the hogs are living beings with the capacity to feel fear and pain. We know the animals have an instinct to live a certain way.
What would a hog confined in a barn say?

The corporations ride on the profit of our lives. Don't they know a pig is a living being with a social structure and an instinct for nesting and care of the young? But a corporation is a unit of thinking. A penal colony.

How does a man rest at night knowing that in the strawless dungeon of pens are all of these living creatures under his care, never leaving except

to die, hardly able to turn or lie down, horror stricken by every opening of
the door, biting and fighting and going mad?
> —MATTHEW SCULLY, *Dominion*

But ask now the beasts and they shall teach thee.
> —JOB 12:7

Will the tortured hog rise up and accuse his tormentors?

Will the last be first?

When will EVERY CREATURE, even the PIG, praise its Maker—when the last hog barn has been wiped from the earth?

I do not have a voice but rely on the one who imagines my voice. If I do not have thought, my voice is heard as though I do.

The first thing I knew was the smell. The ripe bite in the nose that made me alive. The consciousness of burning. A repugnance so deep it scraped raw the inside of the throat.

I was born on a concrete floor to a heaving body held down by a grate. The first sounds I heard were cries unbearable in their intent. Crying to express not pain or distress, but something beyond suffering. I was born into something for which there was only squeal. Almost human at times. How can it be? The instinct to live took hold. I felt my mouth on the teat. Sucking from her heaving belly the boiling milk, the lava of her hopelessness. Litter after litter sucking. That was part of the cry. All this I heard while my mouth worked. I couldn't stop sucking.

Then the teat was taken away. I sucked on whatever I could find—the tail on the pig in front of me, which could not move.

In factory farming, the pigs are weaned weeks before they would be naturally. The desire to suck remains with them. In fact, all their animal instincts are thwarted into a reservoir of relentless, restless longing. The USDA approves what is called "tail docking," in which all but the stub of the tail is cut off, which makes chewing more painful, but at least there is less to chew.

We are in the hog barns of hell. Men are preparing their own hereafter by what they do to us.

We stand in misery. We cannot move. Our joints swell and throb with pain. Our legs break out in sores. We are trapped. We have no hands to hold up in defense but receive the pain given to us. We squeal until our throats choke with grief. How do we make noises to tell? There is a record keeper that comes. The hog farmers do not see. An invisible one who floats over us, taking notes. He writes down what we say. Our pain is recorded. Our agony. Recorded in book after book. The hog-barn farmers do not know. Someday they will read. Their reading will be the hog barn of their own hell. We will testify against them. They will receive understanding.

We wait for our revenge:

For the Lord God said, I send my four severe judgments . . . the sword, and the famine, and the BEAST, and the pestilence.
—EZEKIEL 14:21

The hog barns are an idea. An economic factor. Profit. Making money from the business of farming. A farm group. A corporation. Herd them all together. Think of the hogs as machines.

Sunday, May 2, 1999, St. Paul Pioneer Press
  Claremont, Minn.
   Roger Toquam created quite a stir when he walked into his hog barn last month. Hundreds of young hogs trotted to the edge of the metal divider fences, and a few nuzzled his pants leg as he walked down the long, narrow alley between the individual pens.
   The rural Claremont farmer loved it. That's what he likes to see: happy hogs.
   That means his enclosed feedlot operation which houses nearly 4,000 hogs, is working correctly. It also means he can remain on the farm where he and his wife, Rhonda, are raising three boys.
   Toquam is a typical young farmer in the area, he said. Many have built confinement feedlots as a way to keep themselves on the farm.

When he built the first of the two barns, three other farmers, all younger than 30, also built them.

"Working with nature is the best way to put it. I enjoy being outside."

"It was a necessary move," Rhonda Toquam said. "What business sits still?" She asked. "We are no different. We are a business; we are just out here farming. We have to expand and change."

One night a friend who raises hogs under contract suggested the Toquams look into it. They signed up with a Northfield family farm group, and built their first barn in 1993 and a second last year.

Some people who oppose large confinement operations don't understand why they are needed and how good they are, Roger Toquam said. When people hear about a manure spill, they assume it happened on a large feedlot like his.

But Toquam said he doesn't know of any spills from modern operations.

Sometimes something comes over me. A smell of earth. A desire to be out. Some of us go crazy. I chew the tail stub or leg ahead of me as someone chews mine. I eat myself so I will not be here. The disease spreads. They give us medicine in the food. They come into the barns, their noses covered: the disease, the stench of urine.

We believe in hell.

If reincarnation were true, we would be the extermination camp workers beginning our reward.

Surely for our suffering alone we receive the comfort of afterlife.

A righteous man regards the life of his BEAST.
  —Proverbs 12:10

There is a consciousness of animals. A fullness of being is a state hard to

sustain in confinement—beating, torture, mutilation, execution. What
does this suggest to us about ourselves?
    —J. M. COETZEE, *The Lives of Animals*

More than any other institution, the American industrial animal farm
offers a nightmarish glimpse of what capitalism can look like in the
absence of moral or regulatory constraint.
    —MICHAEL POLLAN, "An Animal's Place"

We are your witness. We speak to the Maker for you. Do you think it is not so? Under your comfort is the nearly human sound of the hogs' squeals. The misery and distress. We hunger for release. We have the desire to be non-confined. We are caged. We feel the surge in the muscle to move, but there is no release. We chew the bars that hold us. We chew on one another. Arthritis, rheumatism, the horror of hopelessness.

You shut the windows of your heart. Pull the curtains. Bring in the yard chairs. Lock the door. Hold your noses, plug your ears so you can't hear our cries.

We are called unclean. We've always taken the rap:

The sow that was washed has returned to her wallowing.
    —II PETER 2:22

And the Lord spoke to Moses and to Aaron saying, Speak to the children of
Israel, saying, These are the beasts which you can eat among all the beasts
that are on earth. Whatsoever parts the hoof, and is cloven footed, and
chews the cud, among the beasts, you can eat.
    —LEVITICUS 11:1–2

And the swine, though he divide the hoof, and be cloven footed, yet he
chews not the cud; he is unclean to you.
    —LEVITICUS 11:7, DEUTERONOMY 14:8

I will continue to eat meat. I agree with Michael Pollan in his article, "An Animal's Place," that "people who care . . . should be working not for animal rights but animal welfare—to ensure that farm animals don't suffer and that their deaths are swift and painless."

Come eat of my flesh: pork chop, pork roast, bacon. I am all in all: Berkshire, Cheshire, Chester White, Hampshire, Poland China, Tamworth, Yorkshire.

I can smell
the sour, grooved block, I can smell
the blade that opens the hole
and the pudgy white fingers
that shake out the intestines
like a hankie.
　　　　　—Philip Levine, "Animals Are Passing from Our Lives"

We received their demons and ran over a cliff:

And when he [Jesus] was come to the country of Gergesenes, two men
possessed with devils met him, coming out of the tombs, exceeding fierce,
so that no man might pass by that way. And they cried out, saying, What
do we have to do with you, Jesus Son of God? Are you come to torment us
before the time? And there was a good way off from them an herd of many
swine feeding. So the devils sought him saying, If you cast us out, let us go
into the herd of swine. And he said to them, Go. And when they were come
out, they went into the herd of swine: and the whole herd ran violently
down a steep place into the sea, and perished in the waters.
　　　　　—Matthew 8:28–32

Did not Balaam's donkey see the angel and prevent Balaam from running into it? (Unless she had turned from me, I would have slain you, and saved her alive.) Numbers 22:21–33.

The animals are a part of our imagination. Our humanity. We read our children stories of animals. Once upon a time there was an old pig called Aunt Pettitoes. The stories have been translated into other languages:

Es war einmal ein altes Schwein, und das hieß Tante Feinefuß. Sie hatte acht Kinder: vier kleine Töchter mit Namen Kreuzschritt, Suck–Suck, Nuck–Nuck und Pünktchen; und vier kleine Söhne mit Namen Alexander, Schweinchen Schwapp, Tschin–Tschin und Stumpfi. Stumpfi hatte Pech mit seinem Schwanz gehabt. Die acht kleinen Schweine hatten einen ungeheuer guten Appetit. »Schnuff, schnuff, schnuff, da essen sie! Und wie!«

— BEATRIX POTTER, *Die Geschichte von Schweinchen Schwapp* (*The Tale of Pigling Bland*)

Let them read their children this.

Friday, April 7, 2000, The New York Times
Tar Heel, N.C.

GOLIATH OF THE HOG WORLD

In many ways, the Tar Heel plant—which can process up to 32,000 hogs a day—is an efficient killing machine. Squealing hogs funnel into an area where they are electrocuted, stabbed in the jugular, then tied, lifted and carried on a winding journey through the plant. They are dunked in scalding water, their hair is removed, they are run through a fiery furnace (to burn off residual hair), then disemboweled and sliced by an army of young, often immigrant, laborers.

For those of you who hold the electric prod and use it in the hog pen—for you operators who hold it to the penned hogs longer than needed—it is waiting for you. For you who drop the hog into the scalding tank before it is dead—Don't be fooled: What you do shall be done to you. Injustice causes justice to stick to it as a bill that comes due. There is no escape.

There, the man in rubber boots and bloodstained apron, his hands steaming with offal, hot as pellets of the sun in the kill.

It is our hope we will have revenge. It is our hope we will be the instruments of our own revenge. It is our hope we will be the noisome BEAST that returns to torture them.

I saw when the Lamb opened one of the seals, and I heard, as it were, the
noise of thunder, and one of the four BEASTS saying, Come. And I saw
a white horse; and he that sat upon him had a bow, and he went forth
conquering.

And when he had opened the second seal, I heard the second
BEAST say, Come. And there went forth another horse that was red; and
power was given to him that sat on it to take peace from the earth, and
that they should kill one another.

And when he had opened the third seal, I heard the third BEAST
say, Come. And I beheld and, lo, a black horse; and he that sat on him
had a pair of balances in his hand. And I heard a voice say, A measure of
wheat for a penny, and three measures of barley for a penny.

And when he had opened the fourth seal, I heard the voice of the
fourth BEAST say, Come. And I looked and, behold, a black horse, and his
name that sat on him was Death, and Hell followed him. And power was
given to them over the fourth part of the earth, to kill with the sword, and
with hunger, and with death, and with the BEASTS of the earth.

—Revelation 6:1–8

Your squeals of fear will be almost hoglike.

Look at the barns from the air in your planes flying over. Are they not lined
up on the hills like patterns of DNA? They are a record. Some day when you wonder about your own torture, this will be shown to you as witness.

What if you never got out of your plane seat?

We cry out to die but there isn't a way.

And they say to the mountains and rocks, fall on us, and hide us from the
face of him that sits on the throne, and from the wrath of the Lamb: For
the great day of his wrath is come, and who shall be able to stand?

—Revelation 6:16–17

You will meet the hog barns you create. They will be
yours.

Where does the evil of hog barns come from? From within? From without?
From both? From economic forces. From the unwillingness to see. I do not believe

in an amoral world, despite the evidence of cruelty in humans, and in the animals as well when they hunt and devour one another. I have even read of a new experiment trying to rid the hog of its *suffering gene,* so it can abide the torment of confinement. What humanity gene has been removed from the owners of the confined animal feeding operation, not to mention owners of chicken barns and the animal experimenters? How can anyone who realizes what we do to animals, much less to one another, not see that humanity needs a savior, a propitiation?

My perspective here is biblical, based on a book written in Hebrew, Greek, and Aramaic by at least forty authors, over a period of 1,600 years, rowdy, inconsistent, open to interpretation, yet with a coherent reality that we are under God with some sort of responsibility for our behavior, for which we will have to answer before the judgment seat. There is a standard that is being violated here in this country that calls itself a Christian nation (at least some call it that). (There is more than one standard being violated, but the focus here is hog barns.) I pray to the Maker, "Take your crowbar, lift the roof off those sheds. Walk through the barns with a respite from their suffering. If you do not like them, send them over a cliff swiftly to their deaths."

At worst, I think the barns will continue to move across the earth until the Lord returns with his crowbar.

> They cry out with a loud voice, saying, How long, O Lord, holy and true, doest thou not judge and avenge our blood on them that dwell on the earth?
>
> —Revelation 6:10

What did we do to get here?

And yet a little season.

Maybe you shall be hogs. Are there not animal transformations?

Think of Nebuchadnezzar grunting with the BEASTS in the field (Daniel 4:32–33).

See the truckload of pigs, suffocated in the heat of a barn when the fans went out?

> They shall hunger no more, neither thirst any more; neither shall the sun

light on them, nor any heat. For the Lamb who is in the midst of the throne
shall feed them, and shall lead them unto living fountains of waters; and
God shall wipe away all tears from their eyes.
—REVELATION 7:16–17

How much like prophet profit sounds.

In short, the things I did were done. I was born. I suffered.
I died. I became bacon. The cries and moans and intense suffer-
ings were carried in the meat. Whoever ate it would eat sorrow
and desperation. It would stir the belly. It would rise in them like
a hot pellet to the brain.

I am pig therefore I am.

Afterword

In July 2000, I visited a swine barn at the University of Minnesota, St. Paul campus. (With a hot potholder to my face because of the smell that burned my nose.)
"What have they done that their punishment is so severe?" I thought as I left. They are
condemned prisoners in cages the size of their bodies, unable to turn or walk. The
pigs that go to market live only six months. The sows used for reproduction live
three years; after that they are less productive.

Thanks to David Schmidt, who took me through the barn. When I asked
what could be done, he said, "If pork eaters demanded pork not raised in barns—if
they would pay more for that pork. Pig barns are the cheapest way to produce pork.
A small farmer can't compete with the corporate farms or farmer who uses the
barns. As always, the bottom line is economic."

What have they done to deserve this? Is the question that stays with me.

Recently, I stayed in a motel on the edge of an interstate. I couldn't sleep for the
sound of passing traffic. I thought of the hog barns I've passed, lining I-35 in
Iowa.

On my way back to Minnesota from Missouri, in December 2000, I pass a sign, *Hog Factories Poison Iowa.*

There are more signs each time I travel I-35.

Politicians take note. Hogs don't vote.

In the newspapers recently I have noticed more editorials and articles on the hazards of air and soil pollution around hog farms. I think they will continue to increase. In bookstores, I have noticed more books on the subject.

TURNING SLOWLY NATURE

Gii–pakweshkaag I'iw Aki

Anooj iko ingii-inaajimotaag a'aw mindimooyenh. Nashke gaye imaa mazhii'iganing nibaawaad iidog aabiging. Miziwe ko gii–pimi-ni-baawag anishinaabeg, baa-mawinzowaad, maagizhaa gaye baa-wewebanaabiiwaad, baa-daawaad sa go gaye. Gaawiin wiikaa bezhigwanong gii-ayaaiiwag. Mii eta go gii-pimi-goziwad, anooj igo izhi-goziwaad.

Miish iidog imaa nibaawaad imaa, mii imaa mazhii'iganing ezhiwiindeg, gaa–izhi–gichi-animikiikaanig giiwenh, gichi-nichiiwa-dinig giiwenh. Mii sa giiwenh ezhi-wenda-go-aabiji-waasesenig. Mii go ezhi-giizhigadinig. Mii naa iwidi enaabiwaad iidog giiwenh gegoo gaa-aniayaanig gaa-ani-naagwadinig, ezhi-waasesenig. Enda-michaani giiwenh, enda-ginwaani, zegiziwaad giiwenh enaabiwaad aaniin ezhiwebak ani-daadobiinig, akiish i'iw, aki iidog i'iw, animi-ayaanig. Mish giiwenh wegodogwen apane giiwenh iwidi ani-wawaas-esenig apane giiwenh iwidi akeyaa minisaabikong, apane giiwenh inaabiwin eni-inaabiigogoodenig imaa. Miish i'wi gaa-ikidod awegwen a'aw.

Miish giiwenh gweshkoziwaad goda, igg-ayaani giiwenh imaa ziibiins imaa ayaanig, imma ge-ani-izhidaabii'iwewaad. Enda-dimi-ini. Mii ko imaa bimi-aazhogedaa-bii'iwewaad i'iw. Enda-dimiini imaa.

Weniban giiwenh, weniban giiwenh imaa i'iw aki, gomaa go minik gaa-izhi-bak-weshkaanigwen imaa, biinge'endamowaad ingiw anishinaabeg. Aandi gaa-inikaag i'iw ayi'ii? Awegwen dinowa mandioo imaa gaa-maajaagwen gii-ikido ko.

Miish iwidi minisaabikong gaa-izhaad. Ayaamagad-sh igo geyaabi i'iw. Mii imaa gaawiin wiikaa iskaabiisinoon imaa gii-paak-weshkaag i'iw aki.

Mii i'iw gaa-inaajimod a'aw mindimooyenyiban. Mii i'iw minik.

The Land Splits Off

The old lady used to tell me about all sorts of things. It's like this: they were sleeping at Garrison once. The Indians used to sleep all over on their way around picking berries or fishing, living here and there. They never stayed in one place. They just moved along, camping all sorts of places.

When they were sleeping there at the place called Garrison, a heavy thunderstorm came up, a great storm. There was continuous lightning. It was like daylight. When they looked, something visible was moving away in the lightning. It was very big and very long, and they were scared when they saw what was happening, a piece of land was making a wake, a piece of land was moving off. They wondered what was going on, as the lightning continued moving off in the direction of Minisaabikong "Rock Island" (Spirit Island), as it moved off with lightning bolts strung across the sky. She said she didn't know who it was (that caused that).

When they woke up there was a creek there where they would have to drive. It's very deep. That's where they drive across. It's very deep there.

Gone, gone was the land there; a piece of land must have split off there and the Indians were surprised. Where had it gone? I wonder what sort of manitou had taken off from there, she used to say.

It went over there to Minissabikong. It is still there. It is never dry there where the land splits off.

That's what the old lady used to tell. That's all.

"Nookomis Gaa-inaajimotawid, What My Grandmother Told Me,"
Oshkaabewis Native Journal Vol. 1, No. 2, 1990,
American Indian Studies Center,
Bemidji State University, Bemidji, Minnesota

All guests at the Center are maimed, rapt away
from the narcissism of nature.
   FREUND (2nd draft), Anne Carson

THE NEXT SUMMER I am at the Lake of the Ozarks. There are ten thousand lakes
in Minnesota, and I rent a cabin in Missouri near my brother.

On my way back and forth to the lake, I drive sometimes after dark. It's
nine hours from my house in St. Paul, Minnesota, to the Lake of the Ozarks in
southern Missouri. Once I pass Sedalia, the last hour and a half is single-lane
traffic through the Missouri hill country. The last time down, I saw a large truck
turn left from Highway 65 onto 52. I thought it would be slow driving, especially
at night when it is harder to pass. But the truck stayed ahead of me. The moon was
full. It was like we were floating on the lake and I was traveling in his wake. He
knew where he was going, anticipating every bend. It was easier to get across the
night behind him. On the edge of Versailles, he turned into Wal-Mart. I went on
alone, south toward the lake, nearly twenty miles ahead, where I rent the cabin. If I
don't get away from the college in the summer, I become involved in meetings,
especially the Council of Multicultural Affairs. As nature thrives on diversity,
maybe so will an academic institution.

The lake is rural but not isolated. My cabin is surrounded by a hodgepodge
of buildings: one old log cabin, an original; a cedar vacation house in which Harry
Truman once stayed; several new, small cottages with decks facing the lake; several
groups of trailers farther back from the lake, second-tier, my sister-in-law calls
them. There are always people walking by the porch windows where I work, or cars
driving by. I turned the table around to face the wall so I wouldn't be distracted by
the traffic.

It is noisy and cluttered on weekends. People arrive on the gravel road just
outside my window late at night. They come to the lake from Kansas City or St.
Louis after work. There are trawlers out on the lake in the early morning. Then the
jet skis, the speed boats, the pontoons, the deck boats, the cruisers. And of course,
there's Quackers, a bar and restaurant where boats come of an evening and the
bass guitar booms from the woofer.

My brother lives farther down the dirt road, in the white house on the lake, in a row of houses and cabins, some set at an angle, whaperjawed and crowded together for lakefront property, or near-lakefront, as if all rushing together, they stand pushed awkwardly together against the water, not knowing what to do.

I have the weekdays to myself to work if I want. I can walk down the hill to visit my brother in the evening. I can go into Laurie, on Highway 5, for groceries, which is the nearest town. From Laurie, I can go into Versailles or Camdenton, eighteen miles either way. It takes several trips to the stores to get settled.

I found a phone line in the cabin on my first trip. When I returned to Minnesota, I called from my phone to have it turned on. The phone company, I found, was in Oklahoma. I had to give directions to the cabin, which I got from my brother, since the cabin has no address. *In Camden County, from Highway 5, take the lake road 1³/₁₀ miles, turn on a dirt road, stay left past the second set of mailboxes to the brown cabin.* My brother's wife sells real estate. There are seven or eight companies in Laurie, Missouri, population 504. On the weekends, you can hardly turn onto the road for the traffic.

Somewhere in getting settled in the cabin, I hear the birds. I see the mallard with her babies who make their nest under the Kitsons' dock. There's a *busy-ness* out there in the warm, sharp light of the early sun; in the voices that carry across the lake. But I also see the fierceness. There's a stray, feral cat that visits my cabin. I feed it, but it runs if it sees me. On the lake road where I walk, there are four puppies left by a sign, *free puppies.* When they see me walking, they run across the road where cars pass. They want to be petted. They want to be *taken.* They want to belong. How could someone leave them in the yard like that? I don't want pup-pies, but am implicated by the fact that I see them, that they run to me across the road, that I am a part of leaving them there. How long until one of them gets hit on the road by a car?

Yes, nature is at the lake; human nature as well.

My unbelief in nature as the ultimate end is the influence of Christianity. In *The Spell of the Sensuous,* David Abrams says, "Some historians and philoso-phers have concluded that the Jewish and Christian traditions, with their other-worldly God, are primarily responsible for civilization's negligent attitude toward the environing earth." Abrams goes on to say that the Greeks also are to blame for their emphasis on thought or pure ideas beyond the apparent world. So it is both Western thinking and the Judeo-Christian proclamation, *Have dominion over all the earth* that have prevailed in my thinking, though native awareness also is there.

There is great diversity within all cultures. It is true with the Native Americans. Mine is not the dominant perspective. I hear native thought. The earth is a living being, capable of being damaged, even killed. We have polluted rivers and caused the extinction of some species. We have taken the natural habitat of animals, and continue to do so, leaving them desperate. Nature is a teacher and guide, sometimes in what *not* to do. There are steadfast rules: what I do to nature, I do to myself. But for me, nature contains both heaven and hell. It is a rubber stamp, a postmark of its travels, indicating where we are headed also. Nature is not to be idealized but to be reckoned with. I've killed two brown spiders in the cabin. I know what their bite can do. Each morning I see there's one less baby duck in the line that swims out from beneath the dock behind the mother mallard. The snakes or raccoons or cat gets them. There is savagery and cruelty in nature. The rabbits lose their babies too.

Isn't that the nature of history also?

My brother is a meat broker. He works from his house on the lake. He carries the same feelings of hurt as I do: a people separated from what we were by a father who said we would live in this world. We both have a need to be alone. To hold back our hurt. To not feel the past. To be. It's an unspoken heritage. A past that is past. The land is something that can never return. The Cherokee removal was several generations ago, but a sense of what is missing remains. What is lived without.

There also is the matter of the cattle I pass in the trucks on the interstate in Iowa as I go back and forth between Missouri and Minnesota. They are on their way to be slaughtered, often in fear and pain and misery. The hog and chicken barns are all over the country now. My father worked for a meatpacking plant. I eat meat, so I take part as a cause of the suffering too.

I guess for me nature is an idea I carry from church. Landscape is the created, not the Creator. The Lord is mightier than the waves of the sea (Psalm 93:4). Keep silent before me, O islands, and let the people renew their strength (Isaiah 41:1).

One of God's complaints against humankind in Romans 1:25 seems to be that they worship the created more than the Creator. But sometimes there are scenes in nature to worship. Often, on my way to the lake, I'm still in Iowa in the late afternoon and evening. The low sun floats across the fields, hazy with dust from the farmers plowing or mowing. There is a pristine light, an ethereal atmosphere. The broad fields stretch both ways from I-35 as lush blankets. There are borders of hedgerows and windbreaks, and clumps of trees surrounding farmhouses to stand against winter blizzards. There are flowers along the embankments by the interstate. To me, the land I pass is an image that reminds me of what Eden must have been. A piece of what nature must have been, only what we see must be dimmed over and over from what it once was. I also know the struggle and loss of farmers. Much of the land is owned corporately now. Insects and weeds are hearty, though the fields and groundwater tables have been polluted with pesticides and poisons.

The Bible is lacking in a lot of landscape description. Maybe it is the nature of Christianity. The Christian heaven seems to be described in terms of city, walls, and gates, though a river is there too. There are armies in heaven on white horses, only I see them as eighteen-wheelers, like the truck I followed across Highway 52. *Come ride with me.*

Often, if landscape is described, the biblical land is described in negative terms: the lack of water in the desert, the dry and thirsty land, the earthquake, lightning and thunder, flood, upheaval. And somewhere in the book of Revelation, the stars fall on the earth; the earth is burnt to a crisp.

The opening of the Bible sets up earth: On the third day God called the dry land into being. He said, *"Let the earth bring forth grass and herb and tree."* By the sixth day, God had created animal and man. He said, *"Let the earth bring forth the living creature after its kind, cattle, and creeping things, and beasts of the earth."* My Scoffield Bible says that the Hebrew word "creature" *(nephesh)* is usually translated as *soul.* "In itself, *nephesh,* or soul, implies conscious life. In the sense of conscious life, an animal also has a soul." He adds that, on the sixth day, all animal life was created. *We and they* together. *They* are the ones in the animal barns. *They* are the puppies left by an open road. We have a responsibility to the animals.

And the water, it seems always to have been there. *In the beginning darkness was on the face of the deep. And the Spirit moved on the face of the waters* (Genesis 1:2). The water was there before the light.

It seems to me, nature is an unsaved world. A world groaning for redemption, for release from fear, guardedness, a state of alertness, a predatory state. Nature longs for release. Creation groans for deliverance like the humanity that inhabits it.

> . . . the creation itself will be delivered from the bondage of corruption into the glorious liberty of the children of God. For we know all creation groans and travails in pain together until now.
> —ROMANS 8:21–22

There are spirits, or spiritual forces, over places in nature. One of them presents itself to me in a dream, letting me know to whom the lake belongs. It is a dream of water I have after I arrive at the lake for the first time. A frame of the lake before a yellow sky. Another framed lake, the sky red as a faded canopy. Earlier, I sat on the dock as the sun went down. Maybe the dream is an afterimage of the dusk, foregrounded with tree branches as if curled ropes. What is it besides the spirit of the place? Why did I connect? Something gone long ago? Some residue of an internal landscape? I remember as a child connecting with the land. There were places in the woods I played. Once in a while I pass a wooded place and that old voice speaks, the one I first heard long ago before my native belief was ruined by my fall into Christianity.

I hear the birds, know their fierce hierarchy from watching them in Minnesota where it is blue jay over starling over cardinal over sparrow. Everything scrambling for survival, not mindful of one another, only of an instinct for survival, for self-preservation of species. The will to live, which means eat and not get eaten. At the lake, the smallest, the hummingbirds, seem to be the fiercest. They jump across the air like little toads. They are a plague from the underworld of Pharaoh's magicians. The woodpeckers, with their sharp shrieks, also are at war.

Another morning at the lake, I am awake early. The birds are chirping. It is a busy place, nature. A noiseful place, a vengeful, treacherous refuge, a hideous sanctuary. Fierceness and gentleness, the same mystery and incongruity and impenetrable light. Not exactly seamless, but a setting for man, who is an image of the creator, the purpose of nature's being.

My nephew-in-law is the jailer in Versailles. Now this is *Ver-sails*,

Missouri, not *Ver-sigh.* And I call it *Missourah,* not *Missourie.* I ask why someone gets put in jail. He says child molestation, family violence, drugs. While we're talking, his two children are tossing pieces of bread to the mother mallard and the babies she brings to my brother's dock. Two male mallards swim up for bread also, and she chases them away. *"They're mean,"* my sister-in-law says. *"Would they hurt the babies?"* I ask. *"They could,"* she answers.

There's a Pima song, *I take the warm parts of the mountain and I climb.* It's not the physical mountain but the living part, the idea of it—the abstraction—the *spirit* of mountain. It's the landscape of the imagination. An internal landscape; thought more than nature. A landscape known by the ideas it creates. An abstraction rather than the concrete. It also is a moving sense of landscape, a passage over the land. Temporary residency: I-35 south through Minnesota, Iowa, and Missouri to I-70 in Kansas City. East on I-70 to Highway 65 south. Highway 65 south through Sedalia to Highway 52. Highway 52 east through Cole Camp, Stover, and Versailles to Highway 5 south. Highway 5 south through Laurie to the lake road. Keep left to the brown cabin. With two stops for gas, one rest stop, and another for a burger to go. Just under six hundred miles. When I add up the mileage, I get different numbers: 584 or 587 or 597. The largest number comes when I get off I-35 in Des Moines for gas and can't get back on because of highway construction and have to drive through town to the next entrance ramp to the interstate. It's a long way, whatever the mileage.

Turning slowly nature, the jet ski spank-spanks the water. There is the possibility of the dream. The subconscious where perception and idea are assembled and appear together as image to face the other. A looking at a dream, an image of road where I had traveled, imposed on the lake, the trees foregrounding the water, nature as second tier, turning to what is behind, moving nature back, placing it back on the shore from the water.

Those spirits have come to live in a certain place, as I have. They picked their places out, maybe fought over them. They let me know who is above me at night. They are possessive, holding to their place. In them power takes form. The earth is a place to make choices that lead in certain directions. The mystery of those choices remains entwined and trapped by hanging branches and vines.

Getting back to the curled ropes in my dream, during another trip, the peripheral vision of the side mirror on my car catches the curved back window. Maybe that was the curve of branches in my dream. The afterimage in my large rearview mirror connected with branches. The mirror connected to the lake, which of course is mirrorlike.

What am I thinking? Imagination exhibits nature. Nature exhibits imagination. Another evening on the dock, I see the waves from a passing boat curve toward the dock; the water is streaked with shadows in the low places between the waves, with lighter water on the peaks of the waves. I think again of the tree branches, their curved forms connecting with the lake as they did in the dream and in the car's rearview mirror. I think of the run-on of seemingly unrelated images: metal, mirror, water, curved forms, and the complexities of the ways in which they intersect. It's the unconscious that deals in the relatedness of things. Nature as idea, as the actual, as the shape of the idea, and the curve of things toward their own end. It's a matter of the perspective from which things are seen.

I take the warm parts and I climb. If there are mountains in southern Missouri, they are low mountains. The Osage River, dammed in the 1930s for the lake, was in a gorge, and the hills are steep. There are cliffs that rise from certain channels of water. In the thinking of what nature is, turning it slowly through thought until it appears as an image in a rearview mirror, a curved window, a tree branch, the image over and over, for miles and miles, until it is one. The source. That warm and living part. I climb to its meaning. Its holy source.

There is a fluidity on the lake besides the water. A boat doesn't have a road to follow. Its wake spreads across the lake and rocks the dock where I sit. There is a motion in the trees, in the sound, in the momentum of a motorboat crossing the water. The old docks creak; they bray like Missouri mules harnessed by the waves as the boats pass.

A jittery blue-black mud wasp hits the screen.

The woodpecker knocks.

During the summer, the heat grows *moveless,* like a child's game of statue. Somewhere on the earth I know it is cold, will be cold again. In the still heat, the birds find cause to chirp; their noise is covered by the drill of the old air conditioner that I turn on in the afternoons. There is an amazing calmness, a knowing, in the center of nature, for all its savagery and *wiliness.*

It is *that,* that is.

WHEN THE BOATS ARRIVED

SOME OF MY ancestors came from Europe on boats. Others were already here when the boats arrived. I have spent a lot of my writing examining the Indian part of my heritage that came through my father. The white part didn't seem to need definition. It just was. Is. And shall be. But what does it mean to be part white? What does whiteness look like viewed from the other, especially when that other is also within oneself?

I can say whiteness is the dominant culture, for now anyway. Or I can say I was taught that whiteness gives definition instead of receiving it. It is the upright. The unblemished. The milk or new snow. It is the measure by which others are measured. There's nothing off center in it to make it aware of itself as outside or other. It doesn't need examination or explanation but is the center around which others orbit. It is the plumb line. Other races/cultures/ethnicities are looked at in terms of their distance from whiteness.

Whiteness is a heritage I can almost enter, but I have *unwhiteness* in me. There is something that is not milk or new snow. I am a person of part color. I can feel my distance from whiteness. There is a dividing line into it I cannot cross. But neither can I cross fully into the Indian, because I am of mixed heritage.

When I look at my white heritage, it is as fragmented and hard to pinpoint as the native side. My mother's family came from England and Germany. They settled in Pennsylvania, then Virginia, and finally the Missouri/Kansas border. What do I know of them any more than my father's family? The European part of the family were practical, middle-of-the-road people. They got their work done. They didn't say a lot about it. They were fair-minded and tenacious. They were church-goers and voters who migrated from the farm to the city in my parents' generation. They educated their children and died without much ceremony.

As for the white culture I saw in my mother's family—they served Canadian bacon every Christmas Eve, which my father brought from the stockyards where he worked. I received an Easter basket on Easter. I got a sparkler on July Fourth. But that hardly defines culture.

I can look at the whiteness in my mother's family and say there was a determination, a punctuality, a dependability. There was a sense of Manifest Destiny, which was another tool for dominance. There was a need for maintenance and responsibility. A sense of a Judeo-Christian God. A holding to one's own. There was a need to be goal oriented. To make use of resources.

There also was opportunity to do all these things.

Who can say what will happen to whiteness as people of color become the majority in the new century? Who can say what will happen as the cultures of the minorities deepen and the white is mixed with others and gets harder to define? Can white culture continue to be defined by its lack of ceremonies? Its Elvises and White Castles? Its harbor of ideas? Will it continue to invent its inventiveness? Will it continue to thrive?

I guess I would define white culture as industriousness without over-whelming tradition. It doesn't seem to have anchors but slides past others into port. Into the port it invented, after all.

IN–BETWEEN PLACES

There came another letter. "Look, Noah, you need to send out the birds in pairs to see if the world is drying."

A ZAPOTEC STORY OF THE FLOOD

OFTEN I WRITE about my own heritage, white and Indian, as an outsider to both. Or as a mixing of both. Or as something that was put away and found to be different than before it was gone. These crossings of cultures are what Gerald Vizenor calls *transveillances.* They are passages not necessarily of choice but of necessity. Afterwards there are dryings, the cultural interpretation of texts.

In an old Zapotec story of the biblical flood, Noah received a letter from God at seven one evening. If people didn't go to church, there would be an end to the world. Noah took the letter to the president, who had his secretary read it at a town hall meeting. The people laughed. The flood came. Noah was tucked in his boat with the parroquets, vultures, macaws, hummingbirds, rabbits, deer, coyotes, and burros. At the end of the Zapotec story, another letter comes from God. "Now you can go with your family. There is going to be a smoke for the world to begin again." Noah stepped from the boat. He found a pine tree. From a big hole in it, a person came out. He had survived the flood too. "Then Noah made himself another house and ranch."

I guess this transveillance could be called a Native American midrash, a development of an existing text. And what if Noah were a Baptist? Maybe the flood was his baptism. What if Noah were Pentecostal? And where did the other person come from—the one who stepped out of the tree? Was he the explorer the Indian first saw? Inserted there because another had come bearing the story he appeared in? And what does that interpretation do to the ancient biblical text?

The Bible was retold, and in the retelling someone had to get it down. Still, there are mysteries and openings that words have to make room for. Sometimes language has to flood. Why else would it be there? The dictionary as an ark of language. From which we can step out.

Permutations are rearrangements of something already existing, but what is an arrangement of something that no longer exists except as an implausibility of itself?

Give Me Land, Lots of Land

In the dryings after a flood, there are revisions. In new versions, there are *redrifts* and *transveillances* across cultures. There are reconstructions of the sentence, which I hate when writing because the sentence constructs a way of thinking that does not include the transpositions, the fragmentations, the interjections, the disjunctions. Because in the adjustments, something can be done that is not complete, creating new ground after the old was covered, imagining who and what and that we are. A search for alignment and also for disruption. And how can both go both ways at the same time? Calling on the reader to create meaning of course, while giving the inventions of words their say and my say. All that going on at once.

Sometimes transveillance works the other way. Henry Wadsworth Long‐fellow was a transveillancer when he took legends from the Great Lakes region, took out parts, and imported a character, Hiawatha, from the Iroquois. Made a subterfuge and called his story *Hiawatha.* At one time, Haskell Institute, a real Indian school in Lawrence, Kansas, had its real Indians play emblems of them‐selves in a traveling production of *Hiawatha.* Making misrepresentation an actual truth of itself.

And, of course, there are many forms of transveillance or misrepresenta‐tion. The Cherokee transveillance is different than the Dakota or Navajo trans‐veillance. The various misrepresentations within the various transveillances are different. My transveillance is different from my father's transveillance, which is different from my brother's, which is different from my grandmother's. My children and grandchildren's transveillances will be different from mine. My transveillance twenty years ago is not my transveillance now.

If narrative style is a vehicle that carries its fragmented history, then I guess the vehicle should reflect its cargo. It should have open places to let in air. Furthermore, the variableness of fragmentation also is survival. As I say in an earlier book of essays, it's not the stories themselves, but the act of storytelling that generates an energy field. It is the field that is vital. It is the fragmentation that actuality holds together / the unheld / unholdable. Or a prose of migrating phrases.

I remember saying I have bookends for which there are no books. Maybe that is a metaphor for Indian heritage. Or being raised at some distance from it. Or having a mistrust of it. Which I learned not only from my white mother, but from my Indian father as well—who kept it at arm's length. I guess because he didn't want to face the loss. And eventually didn't know the loss he faced.

My father worked for the stockyards in several Midwestern cities. Maybe the transfers provided a shifting meaning / a deflection. A cattle transporter that spaces the structure of writing written in pieces. This cattle-pen writing shows up in my books, which often are in short sections because the space between things is as much as the things the space separates.

It's like a section of fence with a gate that is a sentence with two phrases hooked together by a central phrase that opens either way. The barest hinge of connection between. As if we brought all Europeans into one group and called them a name they were not. (Not only is Indian a misnomer, Columbus thinking he was in India, but it lumps the diverse indigenous people into one lump.)

The land, give me land, lots of land spoken open. But even openness is sectioned. There's a movie theater where I live where small lights are transformed into stars that twinkle on the ceiling. It's a simulated sky. For the simulated place all screened up with those opening gates. A cultural history known by the reading instead of being told the actuality of oral tradition. Now it is passed on by the shifting impacts.

Land of Lots

The mix of *in-between* I've experienced is not located directly on or in a border place, but crosses at *sidebands,* turned different ways and intersecting at various points. The result is a sense of *dislocations,* moveable geographies, a sense of *places* somehow woven together yet none complete on their own.

Language, more than place, defines and shapes us. Language is the shape of all that is. At the center of language is the ability, the power, to remember, to name. How could a people begin to speak in another language that is at once dissimilar in its structure of thinking? Maybe that is the root of the displacement I feel, which is a displacement of meaning also.

I am from a language that shifted meaning to another; meaning I now speak something that is not the something the people I came from spoke, or some of the people anyway. These lines are not clear.

Some native tribes believe that land shapes language. But it seems to me more that it is words that shape the land and one's identity upon the land. The European immigrants must have believed that. That's why they insisted the Indians speak English. If they knew the Bible they brought with them, they knew it says the worlds were formed by the word of God making the visible from the invisible (Hebrews 11:3). It seems the Bible also begins with God speaking the world into being. Also, in the Gospel of John, God is *word;* without which there was not anything made that was made.

What happens when that language becomes broken, portable, migratory, and transmutes and disappears into another? My father's Cherokee mother was illiterate. She spoke English, but it was the place she was not from. I remember the lostness or hollowness in her that I also carry, though not to the same degree. Where did she keep her old language? In the woods behind the house? Did she let it go? I don't remember hearing it from her.

Language is our way of knowing the world, of constructing the meaning that enables us to function. Language orders the world and one's place in it. Native American boarding schools were effective in sidetracking identity because they prohibited the speaking of one's native language. It was meant to aid assimilation, but what it did was to deconstruct the native and what that uncovered was the *lostness* of humanity without its root language. It also uncovered the ill-fit of the replacement language that did not carry the meaning of the culture it had been grafted onto. Anyone who has worked with translation knows the difficulty. There are not always ways to say what needs to be said.

In grade school, I had learned that Indians hunted buffalo and lived in teepees and wore feather head bonnets. But when we visited my father's Indian people in northern Arkansas, I saw none of that. We were Indian, but not the Indians that hunted buffalo—wasn't that what all Indians did? And there were still other Indians that were not us; they were from India. How many parts were there? Further, the Indian in America had a name that was not ours but was given us by mistake because the someone who named them was lost, thinking he was in a different place than he was.

Even the city Kansas City, Missouri, where I was born, is named after another state in which it is not located, well it's right next to it, but it is not in Kansas, though there also is a Kansas City, Kansas, but I did not live there. And the city of

Kansas City itself is in Missouri on a bluff above the Missouri River. Why isn't it called Missouri City, Missouri?

My name also is not mine. I was named after my Aunt Helen, though I've never been called by that name. When I fill out forms that ask for last name, first name, and middle initial, my name, Diane, is removed. I was born Helen Diane Hall. I was Diane Hall until I married an Irishman named Glancy. Then I had a name from a heritage that was not mine. And even though I've been divorced longer than I was married, it is that name I still carry.

I went to school in the Melting Pot days, and my difference was supposed to melt into oblivion. But it didn't melt. What is culture made of that it endures? Well, language, certainly. But the Cherokee language is gone from me, though I think patterns of its structure remain, overlapping the lapping of those who own the creek. I also think that's why my writing style is fragmented.

Language—culture—identity—place—everything feels crisscrossed. Is it only in America where *manynesses* and *crossed brands* abound? But in the Old Testament, it was the ringstraked cattle that were Jacob's heritage, his wealth. Maybe the diversity is part of America's strength also.

I was not a part of this, or this, or this. I was partially a part of them all. I was not on any page. I was in the margins of them all. That red vertical line along the left side of my lined writing tablet, a Big Chief, I presume, though I'm not sure any big chief would be writing English if he could help it. I knew a vertical horizon. My sense of identity was upturned, set on end, like the strata of bedrock I have seen in the mountains. Where exactly did I belong? What nationality was I? Why was the road always uphill? Why didn't I hear a voice that sounded like mine? Why am I part of something I am not part of? Where does this immense feeling of isolation and aloneness come from?

I have a straight-backed chair my maternal grandfather made, the one of English descent. The seat is woven with strips of bark. It is rough, coarse, uneven, crude. My cultures are like the weaving of that chair. I am made of the sidebands that cross here and there.

I always have been aware of my own shifting focus. I am a whole made up of different, sometimes incongruent parts, sometimes interrupting one another before they reach their conclusion; or the wholeness is erased, or *overplaced* by another. A *braided life* could define the texture. I see my language, culture, identity, as a bricolage, a diverse collation of things *to be used*. Out of the brokenness I found my voice, fractured, moving too quickly from one place to another, forcing meaning from the broken shapes.

MIGRATION AND STASIS IN THE GEOGRAPHIES OF FICTION

(OR, SOME WORDS AS EXPERIMENT)

A STORY IS a migration to a destination. It is conflict and more conflict that moves to crisis and resolution, which is the destination of a story. There is a necessary tension between the vehicle and its cargo, between the vehicle and the road that follows in its wake. The passengers are character change. Their luggage is the epiphany.

In a story about a granddaughter and grandmother, for example, the conflict is evident from the first sentence of the story: *They had quarreled all morning, squalled all summer.* Several pages later, the resolution is apparent in the last sentence: *The girl walked close behind her, exactly where she walked, matching her pace, matching her stride, close enough to touch her granny's back where the faded voile was clinging damp, the merest gauze between their wounds.*

This part is easy.

To get you there.

Fiction is a nomad. A pilgrim through the reformations of faith it takes to get through the overall ride-of-life which the art-of-the-story is.

You see the *variablenesses* already.

But the structure of a story is its stableness (stasis). The four unchanging elements of the story seem to be conflict, which leads to character change, which leads to resolution, which leads to epiphany.

For instance (continuing with the granddaughter/grandmother story):

A girl goes to stay with her grandmother for the summer. The father writes, *Turn in your plane ticket for school clothes.* The girl is mad. . . . *she fled. Just headed away, blind. It didn't matter, this time, how far she went.* The girl finds two bikers. They ride to Grandma's. Ride off again. The grandma gets in her truck (with the dog that has been yipping all through the story). She chases them down. *Give her back.* The girl gets in the truck. The grandma takes her to the cemetery to weed. The bikers show up. The grandma knows these boys mean business. She, the girl, the dog get past them in the truck. Outrun them for a while. The truck gets stuck in mud on an old dirt road. The grandma, girl, and dog run. They hide under a dock. The bikers come. The dog is yipping (we know he won't be still). The grandmother holds the dog underwater. Drowns it. The bikers can't find them and they leave. The women come out from under the dock, carrying the *freight* (not weight) of the dog. They are now friends.

That's Mary Hood's *How Far She Went* (a story which follows the designated routes of named roads and numbered highways—though the same are sometimes both—and is a direct journey to the story structure). You (easily) see how the vehicle arrives at its destination. The conflicts that escalate between the grandmother and granddaughter cause character change (the grandmother decides the granddaughter is worth more than her beloved dog) and the granddaughter sees, for the first time, that she is valued by someone. The resolution is the acceptance of the intrusion of the other into each of their lives. All this provides (carries as luggage carries) the epiphany, which on a basic level is something like *estrangement isn't always permanent.*

Thus, the story is a mode of transformation. A way to get from one place to another, one hopes a place the characters need to get, or if they didn't, a place that follows logically and naturally from the lineup of events.

There are the necessary curves and turns (impediments) in a story. At one point in *How Far She Went,* the grandmother remembers the unwanted birth of her own daughter, the girl's mother. She remembers saying, *"Tie her to the fence and give her a bale of hay,"* making it harder for her to accept this unwanted child of an unwanted child. Yet, through the circumstances of the story, the grandmother is able to sacrifice her beloved dog for the granddaughter. And the granddaughter, who hated her grandmother, now gets in line behind her.

With their baptism in water under the dock, the granddaughter and grandmother are reborn into new life, which is a new relationship with each other. The *doggedly* life was dead (though didn't the grandmother love it?). Thus, the epiphany is the delivery of something arrived—*life from death,* which is central to the hope of humankind.

There are other elements to the story: the action of plot. Tone. Speed (pacing). The tightness of the elements moving to a common end. The common end itself (toward which elements move), which opens to needed answers. There are, after all, many possibilities in a piece of luggage (different versions or interpretations of a theme, which also can provide different epiphanies for different readers).

There also is the element of spirit, or the spirit–of–being, in a story. Or the redefinition (I hope) of the story as *something living or something–that–lives.* An agency that the vehicle of the story is.

The art of the story is the generative force of storytelling, a need that is everywhere, like air. An old word for breath is the voice as it *tells story.*

The story is a process of an irresolvable need to *tell,* irresolvable other than in the telling and telling of stories.

Stories are old gatherers collecting twigs for cave fires. They ignite from one another. They burn in many ways.

For instance, I was reading a paper a colleague, Roy Kay, had written on Chinua Achebe's *Things Fall Apart,* when I came across one of the Igbor stories. Soon, I felt the shaking of story into stories, or possibilities, or ideas for further stories. I felt the generative force that story is.

The Igbor story is a long story about Tortoise, but to make it short, a turtle asked some birds if he could fly with them to their feast in the sky. The birds agreed, lending him some of their feathers from which he made wings. When they got to the feast, the turtle said that there was a custom of taking new names for a feast. The birds had never heard of this, but they agreed. The turtle named himself *All of You.* When they sat down to eat, the turtle asked the hosts, "For whom is the feast prepared?" The hosts answered, *"For all of you."* The turtle then eats all the food. The birds, angry, take back the feathers, and the turtle falls from the sky. The birds tell the turtle's wife that he is coming. Set out some things on the ground for him, they say. When the turtle falls, he crashes into the things, and his shell shatters into many pieces.

This story of the turtle, itself, shatters into any number of explanatory tales: Why does the turtle's shell look *cracked?* Why is it *half* of a ball? Because at one time the turtle wanted to fly (this was when the turtle was still as round as a ball). He asked the birds for some feathers, which they lent him. But the turtle didn't fly as he should. He bumped into the birds. Took up too much room. Didn't look where he was going. The birds took back their feathers, and the turtle fell from the sky. His ball (orb/sphere) broke in half when he hit the ground. (That's also why the turtle's shell looks cracked.)

The turtle story also could be one of pride: The round turtle, proud of his roundness, presented himself to the Maker as a moon or planet or star—something far beyond that which he was. Since he wasn't capable of being as celestial as he thought, he fell back to earth.

In Igbor's story, the *things* on the ground the turtle falls against could also be the complications the characters must *fall* against in a story. (Not only an unwanted daughter, but an unwanted granddaughter who begins the same life-style that got her mother into trouble, we assume. But now the grandmother has a chance to do something about it.)

Further suggestions for other combinations of stories embedded in the turtle story continue to emerge from Igbor's story of the Tortoise. The art of writing the story is, in part, a conversation with other stories. From one story, other stories are constructed:

At one time, the turtle was not round at all, but flat. But he wanted to be round (as the moon). He asked and asked and never quit asking the Maker to make him round. The Maker agreed, but the turtle wouldn't be quiet. He kept pestering the Maker until the Maker made him round as the moon, but it was only the half-moon the turtle looked like, because he was impatient. The turtle wanted to be like the moon, but he wouldn't wait until the sun covered the whole surface. So the turtle became the darker half.

The turtle or Tortoise shows up in countless folk stories. Sometimes a story circles back and picks up older stories, or fragments of an older story, at the same time it travels forward. In a Native American creation myth (of the Cherokee as well as other tribes), mud was brought from the floor of the ocean and placed on the surface to dry (where it cracked as it dried). The dried mud became the turtle's back, which became our continent. America is called *Turtle Island* by the Native American. It is the basis of our foundation. (Was not dry ground found in the water in *How Far She Went?*)

Thus, the parts of a story interact, showing up at various times in various places, according to where they are needed (called by circumstance).

The purpose of a story often is the explication of our human condition. (Maybe the origin of all stories is the beginning of Genesis: *Let there be light.*) It is the reason stories break into ideas for further stories that can be twisted and applied to various destinations. From big ideas, little ideas begin to form, which themselves grow large and break again. That is the part of the story that is the *something–that–lives*.

A voyage, then, is the vernacular of the story. (A nomad, as I said.) Sometimes containing a story about story (within story). Meaning embedded in its reason for being.

A clumping of marks on a turtle's back. A writing that *makes story*. The vehicle that carries the cargo of meaning (both the freight and weight). So a turtle could say a number of things (however many things need to be said).

The props of language are often in its *resonations*.

In New York, in 1999, I saw a play called *The Weir*. It's a story of four patrons in an Irish pub telling four ghost stories: Little people knocking on the door. The ghost of a woman on the stairs. The ghost of a man in a cemetery. A daughter calling on the phone after she is dead. And I wondered where was the basic *whereness* (the plot–drive, the conflict/resolution, the mix of the elements together)? Now this was a play, not a story, but a story nonetheless in script form. Each character met his or her limitations and found it was necessary to continue with them, or there were small changes and/or epiphanies for each.

But, I thought, maybe the story was in language. Maybe the story was in the concept of the weir:

A weir is a dam built across a river to regulate the flow of water, to raise the level upstream for farmers. A weir is also an enclosure of stakes set in a stream to catch fish.

The weir could be the bar (the setting) itself, where stories are caught in the imagination. The weir also is the stories themselves.

It is the carrier as well as the carried. Maybe the story is in the way the weir acts as vehicle as well as content (cargo) of its own cause, in the way language has to be used to talk about language. A generator of a big bang on a small–bang level in the intrinsic rumblings of the creative process.

A story is a combustion through written language, those sticks of words rubbed together. Language is an agreed-upon event. A carrier of meaning in sound or the silence of black flecks of writing on the page, the fish caught in a cage.

In this (con)text, our first cries are ourselves answering ourselves. Yes. A story answers the "outness" (what is out there), but mainly the "inness" in the vastness of our being. It turns to an infiniteness that opens when the variables resonate and get us linked to others. That's the art of the story.

The grammar (sentence structure) = the fish-catching enclosure of stakes in a stream.

After the play, I went to the Metropolitan Museum in New York, and there was an actual fish cage in a *Native Paths* exhibit: a rattle trap through which the stream runs, letting fish in but not out. The way a story is picked up by the real (when all the story elements run through a story). There's an old magic of *speaking into being*. When you get it right, the story enters real life.

In the looseness and rigor of language, David Abrams, in *The Spell of the Sensuous,* quoting the literary theorist Merleau-Ponty, quoting another theorist, Saussure, mentions the *weblike* nature of language, a construct built by construct, an interdependency, a living, changing field of action. Which the story is, re-verb-erating in all directions as a stone (stasis) dropped into a (migrating) stream.

Nature writes with the return of the seasons. The clouds in various formations, sometimes even absence of formation, and all the storms that come from them. The scrawl of leaves, the fall and return of them. The same pattern in *change-a-bell-ness.*

At the core of writing is the road map for the movement of travel.

A bell ringing.

The story is an uncovering (because the larger mind, the one that under-stands this art-made-to-look-like-life, can get to the metonymy of being which art is).

The art of the story takes the rock off the mouth of the well (when all the sheep are gathered). (*We cannot roll the stone from the well's mouth, until all the flocks are gath-ered together* [Genesis 29:8], though Jacob did.)

Jacob was at the well in the desert when he saw Rachel coming. He rolled the rock from the mouth of the well so she could water her sheep. Jacob wanted to marry Rachel, but Laban, her father, tricked him. Jacob agreed to work seven years for Rachel, but when Jacob unwrapped his bride, he found Leah, Rachel's older sister. He had married the other daughter first. He had to work another seven years for Rachel, the desired one (Genesis 29).

A story is regulated by a speed limit to hold you in it.

A story is a life-giving force. The passing of a vital survival force before your eyes.

Depending on the resourcefulness of the position of the hearer to survival.

A metaphor of our thinking is what writing is.

The exactness of story along a line to critical inquiry.

A migration of the imagination. A subversion of learning the art of story by afterthought (the process of *rewriting the already written*).

You know these old questions a story has to answer (the stasis):

What does the character want? (Jacob wants Rachel.) What keeps the character from getting it before he gets it (or doesn't)? (Jacob discovers Leah instead of Rachel the morning after the wedding.) (But what is Leah but a preliminary draft of the final version?)

In my own work, I sometimes rely on experimentation in the writing process, and on the redefinition of the story as a *being*. (In native literature, the landscape, or setting, is often cast as a living being, a character, paralleling what is happening in the story. It's the reason I often go to a *place* for the *story* I'm writing.) When a story is defined as *being*, there are possibilities of transformations in its elements—the possibility of one thing becoming another. It has its roots in native stories of animal transformations and conjurer's magic.

It gets back to the concept of a weir. A metonymy of water to a cage (water is not a direct part of the cage, but the cage is not a cage-in-action without the water).

Writing is a theoretical looking–for–a–garage for the vehicle of transportation that a story is.

A story is a structure of thought that makes it possible to travel where there is no road. An experiment to see how far she (the language of the story structure) can go.

MUD PONIES

When the wall is fallen, shall it not be said unto you, Where is the daubing with which you daubed it?

    Ezekiel 13:12

mud dauber n: *any of various wasps (esp. family Sphecidae) that construct mud cells in which the female places an egg with spiders or insects paralyzed by a sting to serve as food for the larva.*

    Webster's New Collegiate Dictionary, 10th ed.

I keep a small mud dauber's nest in my collection of natural objects. I don't remember the house it came from. Probably it was in Oklahoma. But I think of the pieces of mud the mud dauber carried over and over, bit by bit, until the nest was shaped. Then the work of catching and stunning insects, packing them into the chambers. I could transfer that image to my grandmother's quilts, as well as to writing.

When did the monotony of her world roll back and did she receive the visions for the quilts she made? And where did she get the material for the squares and triangles in her patterns? I know she used our old clothes, but I don't remember any of us wearing the florals, plaids, prints, stripes, and checks in her quilt pieces. Who wore the mustard-and-brown plaid? Who wore the rose-and-turquoise stripes? The polka-dots? The fleur-de-lis? The maroon-and-fuchsia pajama stripes? The purple berry print? The brown-and-white windowpane print? The turquoise emblems on yellow-umber? The alternating rows of tiny hexagons? Maybe she shopped in some exotic, far eastern market. And what pulled her back to Kansas? The frozen winters they had? The blast of summer? Chicken house, barn, fields, cellar, house, the stump where she beheaded chickens. My grandparents were together night and day on their Kansas farm, year after year, never apart unless he was in the field, and then not much out of shouting range. They were in it for the long haul, Forest and Myrtle Wood. Five children, one died in childbirth and nearly killed her too, she later said, but they kept at it, trying to get it right for three more daughters and a son.

And where did my grandmother get the patterns for her quilts? The names of some I looked up in my old book, *American Pieced Quilts* (Jonathan Holstein, Viking, 1972): *Robbing Peter to Pay Paul* and *Baby Blocks,* those rows of cubes stacked together that also look like chevrons if you see them another way. Others of her patterns seemed made up. Three of her quilts hang on my walls in Minnesota. My grandmother's quilts are like large hot pads. They were used as blankets against the cold, of course, but they were hot pads against the plainness of the Kansas prairie. In the distance beyond the fields where she never went, in the repetition of stupefying chores, in the dizzying heat that bleached the prairie dry and brown in summer, in the frozen winters that nearly wiped them out, there must have been a need for something to hold against it. In the slap of wind against the house, in the windlessness, her quilts must have whacked their way into the world.

I often think of the work it took, of how much is involved in getting where you want to go and how long it takes to get there, when you come from nowhere and have a long way to go, and no one but yourself to get you there. I think of the constant leaks, the filling in around the missing parts. But that sort of *fixing* always is with us. In Exodus 2:3, Moses' ark of bulrushes was daubed with slime and pitch. In Genesis 6:14, Noah's ark was pitched. I guess I could say her quilts were having the cracks (some of them) filled with work (some of it anyway). Chances are the vessel would float.

I recently had an e-mail from a student asking if she could take a writing class as an independent project, which meant no class attendance, no reading of the material, no critical input on the work of her peers during workshop, and more importantly, no critical comments from them on hers. She just writes and I read it and make comments.

It may have been she who asked if it were possible to speed-read in my Native American literature course. I said I didn't think so. The literature is usually convoluted with many narrators and no straight narrative, with a lot going on in the subtext. It is hard enough to read slowly. The word that came to mind about her was *shortcut.* Maybe one of the purposes of life is the acceptance of the work it takes.

There's a Pawnee story called "The Boy and the Mud Ponies":

A long time ago there were no horses. A boy had a dream about ponies.
He knew their shape and how their tails and manes looked. He made

two ponies from mud. He took the ponies to the creek and pretended
they were drinking. He took the mud ponies to the good grass to eat. One
night, the boy had another dream. He dreamed he heard singing and he
remembered the song. When he woke, he sang the song. In his singing, the
mud ponies came alive. That's how the horse came to the Pawnee. (The
Pawnee Mythology, *George E. Dorsey, Carnegie Institute of Washing-*
ton, Washington, D.C., 1906.)

I often remembered my grandmother when I wrote for years without publication, but I kept daubing. Kept wanting publication. I kept singing my work a
song to live.

Now these are some of the mud ponies I saw. Writing that is daubing,
that is as significant as the vessel (the life) it daubs, though one meaning of daub
is crude, unskillful. To reflect the broken context. The contradictory. To walk in
two worlds. To walk in none. To straddle a mixed-blood heritage. To write about
faith/tradition. To break up paragraphs. Sentences. To work with the cohesiveness
of dis-cohesiveness. To remake a mud nest into various genres. Because it takes
a mix of genres to reflect the fragmentation. (There actually was a mud room in an
old house we had—just inside the back door, for hanging coats and leaving boots.)

I've always liked the story of Job in the Old Testament. He lost all his animals, his servants, and his children. His three friends came and offered advice.
Finally, in chapter 38, God asks the friends, Eliphaz, Bildad, and Zophar, *"Where*
were you when I laid the foundations of the earth? Where were you when I shut up the
sea with doors?" After they closed their mouths, the conclusion to the whole story
comes in chapter 42 when Job says, *"I have heard of God by the hearing of the ear, but*
now I see him with my eyes."

Cynthia Ozick writes about Job in an article, "The Impious Impatience of
Job" (*American Scholar,* Autumn 1998). "The ways of the true God cannot be pene-
trated," she says. "The false comforters cannot decipher them. Job cannot uncover
them." In other words, we can make mud ponies, but the dream and the song from
which the horses come do not originate with us. All our daubing, however necessary, is only a part. There always is something other than what we are.

The writing of words takes obedience and patience also. When I'm writing,

I go over and over the words. Sometimes I have to shut my ears to the discourage-
ment around me. I think I am more than I would be without patience. It has been
for my benefit. I think midlife feels solid and grounded because of it.

My daughter, when she graduated high school, wanted to become a lawyer,
after I was divorced and on my own, traveling for the Arts Council of Oklahoma,
knowing there was no way around the hard economic wall we faced. But we bor-
rowed money for the seven years she was at the University of Kansas. She was (we
were) $30,000 in debt when she finished. The student loans were called Sallie
Maes. Piece by piece we returned the money. The loans were paid off in January
1998. She is now a lawyer in Kansas City, Missouri.

> *I called to the Lord and my cry came before him, even into his ears. The*
> *earth shook and trembled; the foundations of the hills moved. There went*
> *up a smoke out of his nostrils and a fire from his mouth devoured; coals*
> *were kindled by it. He bowed the heavens and came down, and darkness*
> *was under his feet. He rode upon a cherub and did fly upon the wings of*
> *the wind. (from Psalm 18)*

I think, too, of the years it took for my son to settle on his teaching
career after the 1990–91 Persian Gulf War. But Daniel prayed three months for
an answer. Israel was in Egypt four hundred years. Noah waited a week closed up
in the ark with the animals, the neighbors taunting him, until it began to rain. Rain
no one had ever seen.

I still have spaces between the boards of the house I'll always have to daub.
A Native American and Christian aesthetic. Writing and teaching. Mother and
self. It is why I have two feet, one for each world. Or I have four more feet by riding
a mud pony. Then (actually) I have six feet. For mud ponies, arks, mud daubers'
nests, mixed genres, mixed heritages and messages.

Daubing has affected my life as a teacher also. I started with various
fractures (*fictures* is the word I first wrote). Working, which is writing the structure of courses, teaching, reading, and commenting on students' papers. All the
other details of teaching. Going over them and over them. Sometimes I'd rather
be reading a book I want to read, or writing, or working with critical theory for the
Native American literature I teach. The multiplicity of its subtexts. The fragmen-

tary decenteredness of its texts. The enormous burden of my writing spreading out into various genres, all in various stages of completion, teaching full time, family responsibilities like so many islands floating in midair; and after all this work, certainly not a recognized name. I think it has taken faith to keep it going. It has been more than I could do on my own.

Gerald Vizenor has a term, *timberline,* he uses in his book *Fugitive Poses,* which I use in my Native American literature course. The term describes our two-sided language. I struggle along his timberline. Of language as meaning and no meaning. All that floats between. Equine language. The stories behind the words behind the voices of the stories. Language as a living being, like the earth, that depends upon a variability of variables and layers of reciprocity. A wobbliness that is always with you.

What lasted after my grandmother's life was over? Her children, grandchildren, and great-grandchildren, certainly. Her quilts, like chambered nests when the wasps moved out. Why did my grandmother keep quilting? Because she chose to. Because she had an inclination for it. The quilts kept coming. The act of daubing. Bed after bed. Wall after wall. It is what she found to do. It's what she made room to do. It's what she had to do or else be open to the ravages. Her quilts were a one-dimensional house for her imagination.

What lasts after all of this is over? The chambered nest when the wasps move out? The words to say what you were, and the words to say the hope of where you are going.

But what will stand when it is over? That's my concern of (past) midlife. Especially on a rough flight back from Austin, Texas, in a windstorm. If my life stopped, what mud wall would stand? Maybe death is the ability to face the same uncertainty that life is. You get into it (like birth) not by choice but by circumstance. Probably what lasts (I hope) is the understanding, the discovery of voice, thought, the spirit that is more than life.

Why do I do this? Because I choose to. Because I have an inclination for it. The words keep coming. The act of daubing. Wall after wall. It is what I found to do. It's what I made room to do. It's what I had to do or else be open to the ravages. I imagine walls that make a habitat for imagination. Things disappear as life moves on. Even though the walls are daubed, other things stay. I know the real horses come from mud ponies. I know a song that makes them live.

I remember walking to my car from behind, when I was loading it for the trip. Its doors open on both sides, held out to me like arms. A biplane, if I opened all four doors. Ready for takeoff.

In my patience I possess my soul (Luke 21:19).

TERRA–COTTA HORSES

WHEN I TOLD my son I was going to China with a stop in Hong Kong, he said, "Don't bring me anything." He had passed through Hong Kong on the USS *Okinawa* during the Persian Gulf War. That was all of it he wanted (see postscript).

Three and a half hours from MSP to L.A. Fourteen hours from L.A. to Hong Kong. Two hours from Hong Kong to Beijing. Halfway around the world. China is shaped like a rooster.

Highway construction is casual. You feel, riding along, that you could get out of the bus and pick up a hoe.

The first word I think of is *squalor.* The chambered, utilitarian, high-rise apartment buildings in Beijing, city of 9.3 million, remind me of the mud dauber's nest I have in my collection of natural objects. Only they are not empty but have glassed-in porches filled with boxes, all kinds of clutter, and what looks like junk. I think of the principle of hog barns applied to people. Other words come: nautilus, Jules Verne's *Nautilus,* murky, underwatery, unfathomable. At the same time, how can China feel dry? China is a mud dauber's nest. Packed dirt. Hard dust. The floor I remember in my grandmother's cellar in Kansas. More people on bicycles and in open-windowed buses than looks possible. The traffic stirs up a haze in the streets. Another word, *dingy,* dim, as if the brightness of unclouded light would be too much. Language, trying to describe the sameness of this difference, goes every way at once. Looping, frenzied, jet-lagged, oppositional language.

A fortune cookie in a Chinese restaurant for tourists says, *The purest pleasures are found in useful work.*

There are places to visit; in Beijing: the Summer Palace with old women sweeping the walks and bare dirt, the Forbidden City, the Great Wall, Tian'anmen Square surrounded by the building-size picture of Mao and the monoliths-of-white-granite government buildings of the People's Republic of China. But what does the Republic have to do with the people? And what is their definition of republic?

Barbara Tuchman has some chilling words in her book *Notes from China* (Collier Books, 1972).

> At a military barracks, I noticed no provision for families. The state pays
> for an officer's home leave or for visits by his family to the post, but apart
> from that, he does without his wife's companionship. After an officer has

served 15 years with a good record, he may apply to have his family live with him.

When I asked about this, an officer replied, "We consider it a happy life to live and work with our friends and comrades of the great proletarian People's Liberation Army."

Young children are sent to boarding kindergarten from which they come home for a one-day weekend.

To eliminate the trouble of cooking, a husband and wife can take their meals at the office cafeteria, the wife at her office and the husband at his.

I wonder if the collective mind causes the squalor. When nothing is yours, you don't want to take care of it like you do when you have ownership, or at least an investment in it. Other words come, lack of diversity. The plague of uniformity. Yet China is a republic. But is it the same *and to the republic for which it stands?* A government having an elected chief of state. A group of citizens entitled to vote for elected officers and representatives, and to be represented by those elected officials and representatives (for redundancy and duplicity of documentation). China has elected officials too: the president, who is head of state, the premier, and the general secretary, who is head of the party. But the problem: China has only one party. China also calls itself a democracy, but it is a tightly controlled democracy with a government-controlled means of production.

In Beijing, the tour group visits the Central Academy of Peking Opera, the Central Academy of Drama, the Chinese Theater Association, the Beijing Music Hall. The buildings are cold, gray, and drafty. It is early October. Heat is not turned on until November 16.

What I begin to miss in China is the song. The imagination. The possibilities. Practicality and vision. Earth and dream. The balance. The diversity of thinking.

The ten-day cultural exchange tour of Beijing and eventually Xi'an, once the largest city and capital of China through eleven dynasties, is mainly theater, though most of the exchange is theirs, dispersing socialism, Buddhism, a variety of political propaganda, and regimentation mainly through bureaucrats. The contrast between possibility and reality is sharp. Often the exchange feels staged, stunted.

Whose idea is this? The people reacted so violently to the emperor, in the process they keep themselves peasants by still working for something they consider greater than themselves: the state instead of the emperor. Freedom to think might create more artists like Gao Xingjian, who receives the Nobel Prize during the tour and lives in exile in France. Oddly, when we ask about contemporary Chinese playwrights, he is never mentioned.

After the plane trip to Xi'an, we visit the Folk Arts School and the Shaanxi Provincial People's Art Theater. We eat a Peking duck at Quanjude Restaurant and a dumpling dinner at Zhuque Restaurant. Hawkers with their wares follow every step. *Postcards one dollar.*

Books to read: Guanlong Cao, *The Attic;* Chang-rae Lee, *The Gesture Life;* Ying Chen, *Ingratitude;* Anchee Min, *Red Azalea;* Ha Jin, *Waiting;* Adeline Yen Mah, *Falling Leaves;* Wang Ping, *Aching for Beauty;* Jung Chang, *Black Swans* (for the brutality of Mao). And, of course, *The Art of War,* by Sun Tzu, written some two thousand years ago, with commentaries ranging over one thousand years. *Required reading for the Marines,* my son said.

In the memoir *Falling Leaves,* when the parents of Adeline Yen Mah threaten to turn her out of the house, she writes, "I had seen babies wrapped in newspaper beside the road and orphans scavenging for food. *Where would I go?"* She asks her parents. China, where the individual is of least importance. China of the unwanted female children. China of the murdered female infants. China with its history of foot binding. Of making indentured servants of young wives. *Have many sons and no daughters.*

Near Xi'an, we visit the terra-cotta warriors at the burial site of Qin Shin Huang, 259–210 B.C., the first emperor of the Qin Dynasty, who united the seven provinces of China then spent the rest of his life building his tomb, which includes the field of buried soldiers. Not all have been excavated, but there are probably six thousand standing (life-size) soldiers, other soldiers kneeling with bows arched, and more than six hundred chariots and harnessed horses ready for battle.

In 1974 a farmer digging a well brought up a warrior's terra-cotta head. He called authorities, and they uncovered the field of soldiers and horses broken in pieces. After Qin Shin Huang's death, revolting peasants knew the terra-cotta soldiers held weapons. They broke into the tomb and stole the swords and spears and set fire to the tomb with its wooden pillars and roof. Only a few have been restored. (Restoration of the terra-cotta horses and soldiers could solve one of China's problems—keeping its people busy.)

If I dig straight through the earth from the burial mound in China, would I come up at *Rocky Mound* in Hume, Missouri, near my grandfather's farm just across the Kansas border? I think of the two geographies. Diametrically opposed east/west.

"Be subtle even to the point of formlessness. Be mysterious even to the point of soundlessness," *The Art of War,* by Sun Tzu. "Your battleground is not to be known, for when it cannot be known, the enemy makes many guard outposts and since multiple outposts are established, you only have to do battle with small squads."

I like the shifting perspectives, the texts open to various applications, the changing assessments. Something like the U.S. Constitution. The commentaries on *The Art of War,* which have been written over thousands of years, read like a Chinese midrash.

In contrast to human strategy in *The Art of War,* the Old Testament God worked with the weakness of his people. God is the one who defeats the enemies. In the tenth chapter of Joshua, for instance, five kings join forces and camp before Gibeon. When Joshua prays for help, the Lord says to Joshua, *"Fear not, for I will deliver them into your hands."* Over and over, in all the battles of Israel, it is God who routs the enemies of his people.

"Attack when they are unprepared. Divide and separate." This is the philosophy behind the biblical Tower of Babel. Otherwise, language invades and lets in otherness and diversity because it is a living entity. On limiting the discursive aspect of language with its interactive qualities, it becomes a separator.

One day during the tour, we travel to the country. Because of the hawkers and their quilts, I think of my grandmother's needle moving like water along an irrigation ditch. Some of her quilt patterns are geometric, cell-like structures, like a wasp's nest. Inside the patterns, there are compact, close quarters. In the country, we stop in a farm village. The houses within their enclosures are like cocoons, cellars, submarines. (*"In China,"* the guide says, *"we eat everything in the sea except the submarines."*) I think of Job during his trials. Maybe the land of Uz could have been in China. The farm buildings are sparse, hard, grim. Corn is drying on the roofs. There are shrines in the fields. The buildings are squat, stone structures with enclosures and pens. A dog of some sort, tied to a post, is barking. There is the usual clutter: a broken shovel, a plastic scoop, a broken stool, various implements of indeterminate origin and use. In the Minneapolis Art Institute, back in America, there's a thirteenth-century painting of a boy leading an ox along a farm path, which I have always liked. I see the same scenes as we travel through the country.

The only exotic I remember on my grandfather's farm was the Chinese checkers game with the points of its star: red, magenta, ultraviolet, blue. I remember the farmhouse kitchen at night, the small haze of light around the kerosene lamp, beyond which the darkness of the universe chewed the corners of the room.

The thought of the Chinese army is chilling. The word "imminent" keeps surfacing. "Military formation is like water. The flow of water is determined by the earth; the victory of a military force is determined by the opponent. A military force has no constant formation. Water has no constant shape. The ability to gain victory by changing and adapting according to the opponent is called genius." Diversity also is genius. It keeps the ship from sinking into sameness. It is the secret of the greater part not known but open to interpretation. So it is with diversity and cultural wars of voices trying to fit together while establishing their own ground.

The mind itself is a diversity, a quilt-work shape of print and color, a splicing, a joining of divergent parts of unlikenesses. A peasant's farm in China, a grandfather's farm in Kansas. The grandmother's quilts, the quilts and quilt-work pieces sold by the Chinese on the streets. (The hawkers and street venders with their quilted vests and bags and coverlets follow us everywhere. Where did I read the Chinese are nonaggressive?)

During travel, I felt this swift turning. This shift in focus. This moving outside the margin when you have been the paper itself, and for them to what? Ruin? Do it differently? Change the margins, the lines, the rules? Dot you out? Say hop over. Step off the page. One of the problems of diversity is to realize you are not the main one.

I notice the contrasts in *The Art of War.* "Those who render others' armies helpless without fighting are the best of all." (I wonder how much technological information the Chinese got from former President Clinton's administration, which the Lewinsky investigation overshadowed.) How do you be protective yet cooperative? The oppositional contrasts in *The Art of War* are startling: fluidity within structure, relativity within solidity. "Victory in war is not repetitious, but adapts its form endlessly." Yet:

> "Military action is important to the nation—measure it in terms of five things (the way [aim], weather, terrain, leadership, discipline)."
>
> "There are three ways in which a civil leadership causes the military trouble."
>
> "There are five ways of knowing who will win."
>
> "There are five rules of military (measurement, assessment, calculation, comparison, and victory)."
>
> "There are five traits dangerous in generals."
>
> "There are six ways to defeat."
>
> "There are five kinds of fire attack (burning people, supplies, equipment, storehouses, weapons)."

I see my grandmother on a mud pony as I travel through China. I feel a storm of mixed heritages, mud ponies, terra-cotta horses, arks, cellars, the Great Wall of China, pagodas, Kansas hollyhocks, grape arbors, mud daubers' nests, tomato vines, windbreaks, rice paddies, water buffalo, a winter row of pines. A bus ride through a foreign land heavy as the grease in my grandmother's gravy. Mysterious, mixed-messaged diversity, full of hopes and disparities and voids, like birds that cannot fly. (*"In China,"* our guide says as we travel between sites, *"we eat everything that flies except the planes."*) Often I sit by myself looking out the window while others talk noisily. Often I daydream.

The restrooms in China are concrete or ceramic squat holes, not always with doors, not always even stalls. The floors of the stalls are usually wet. You carry the urine on the bottom of your shoes, or on the hem of a jacket or bag that touches the floor when you squat. Sanitation is needed as infrastructure. Among the first warnings are, *Don't drink the water. Don't open your mouth in the shower. Rinse your toothbrush in boiled water.* When I see the brownish water in the shower in the first-rate tourist hotel in Xi'an, I understand. The coarse towel and soap have a faint smell of disinfectant. There is little thought given to comfort. How long before widespread disease takes off from this place?

There is something earthy about China, washed of innovation, imagination. It is in need of dusting, cell-like as the cellar on my grandmother's farm in Kansas. Something underground. The dirt floor with a polished sheen, but a dirt floor nonetheless. China is not far from the ground.

Somewhere in our guide's utilitarian information about her country there are traces of stories or myths. Once in a while I hear remnants of what once was: *No one bothered to come to Buddha's birthday party but the animals: rat, tiger, monkey, pig, ox, horse, rabbit, sheep, dragon, snake, dog. That's why the names of the years are given to the animals* (the year of the pig, the year of the snake).

That's what is missing in China: song, which is the map of a country's geographies.

There are other places where I see what must have been. At every temple there are two lions beside the stone stairs. One lion, the female, feeds a cub with her claw. The other lion, the male, holds a ball under his paw. Did the early Chinese know the world was round centuries before the West did? Or was the ball a symbol of something else in the world? Wasn't there an observatory (twelfth- or thirteenth-century) in Jaipur (India) or Mongolia (?) where someone surmised the earth was round?

A collective of Tuchman's comments:

The big issues: *China's struggle to feed and house its people.*

The names that come back: Chairman Mao Tse-Tung. Chou En-lai. Chiang Kai-shek.

All thoughts are flattened into slogans and drilled into the heads of the public.

Intellectuals, artists and writers undergo reeducation and transformation. (*I hear a comment from someone on the tour about how much art was destroyed during the cultural revolution.*)

All cultural and intellectual enterprise serves the Revolution and increases production.

The art of the people describes the dauntless integrity of the proletarian revolutionaries.

The Chinese are used to living with a prescribed pattern of behavior.

As always the foreigner feels inadequate to penetrate the reality.

Nearly thirty years later, Tuchman's description of housing is right on (not the new high-rise apartments, but the old housing low to the ground, much of which was cleared for the apartments): *"The maze of alleys and courtyards are clay houses with dirt or stone floors in which several families sleep, sharing a common bathhouse with other families."* I see the same maze of tile-roofed houses with stones and bricks holding down the roofs. The same neighborhood latrines with their stench that families share. The aged, metal, utilitarian bicycles everywhere.

In China, everything is equal. But what is the definition of equal? We are *equal* in America, but it is a different equal than China's equal.

The next time I see produce, I think of the bare farms from which it comes. The next time I buy something "made in China," I remember the cold, dirt-floored *factories* from which the something came.

It seems to me China's fault lies in squashing the possibilities of language with its language, making words do the opposite of what they should. China absconds language, leaves it a dry geography. But it seems that the former imperial language (before the proletarian) required terra-cotta horses to defend it.

Maybe the final lesson is that all our words crumble—mud ponies as well as terra-cotta horses—before the mystery that language is.

Diversity is disconcerting, upsetting the context, changing the content. It is the song that makes horses of mud ponies on a little bus trip in a foreign place. A little mud bus turning into a plane with its flying-insect wings. The horses on the journey change, but the song, the process of bringing them to life, is the living, diverse, uncertain voice, which China does not allow.

Postscript

August 13, 1990

Dear Mom,

*   . . . We just finished 30 days in P.I. (Philippines) and are heading to Hong Kong for a few days. From there we should hook up with the rest of the 7th*

Marine Amphibious Brigade. I heard (supposedly but not for sure) to the Persian Gulf. I don't know when I'll write next or when I'll get my next mail. . . . Love, Dave

(Saturday morning, August 18, 1990, I opened the St. Paul Pioneer Press to the bold heading, "CRISIS IN THE GULF." Beneath the heading was an Associated Press photo of the flags of several nations in the foreground, and in the background, a ship, under which was the caption: "The USS Okinawa, a helicopter carrier, left Hong Kong with four other navy vessels on Friday to join the growing U.S. force in the Persian Gulf region." I knew David was on that ship.)

Oct 15, 1990
Dear Mom,
. . . . We've passed the "65 consecutive days at sea" mark. Not much to do to pass the time. I have plenty of books now, but it's hard to get motivated to read them sometimes. We're probably not going to get back until February. Thanks for the packages. They really help out. . . . The mail has been slow. It bounces from port to port. Sometimes sitting a week at the ports. It's very pretty at night with all the stars out. We saw some birds the day other day so we're close to land. Two of our Hueys (helicopters) crashed the other day—8 killed. I helped pack one of the pilot's belongings. I knew him so I helped. We have only two Hueys left. I rode in one of the ones we lost two days before the wreck. . . . Love, David

October 30, 1990
Dear Mom,
. . . Well, an unbearably hot ship is getting hotter. We don't know yet what our mission will be over there. They don't know. The troop's morale is down, which is to be expected. . . .

December 1, 1990
Dear Mom,
Everything's going well so far. The waves have been pretty high. We're doing a lot of rockin' but I haven't been too sick. Just a little every now & then.

We still have 15 days before we land. The sea is very pretty and the helicopters are fun to see & ride on. However, that gets old after a while. My guys work hard now and I hope they can keep it up. A couple of them have been getting really sick. I basically work for a few hours, then sleep for a few hours, work, sleep, work, sleep, with eating and working out in between. Meals are pretty good most of the time. We do get to watch videos at night and I've been reading some—mostly my Bible and Spanish book. Well, I need to get this out now or I won't get it out for another 15 days. Take care & God bless. Love, David

Dec. 1990
Dear Mom,
     And then 60 days straight became 75 straight days. And to think I was bored at the 30 day mark. . . .

     (On January 16, I was watching the evening news when I saw the first American missiles fly over Baghdad. Somewhere during that time, I dreamed of David with his hand in the water. Underneath, I saw the fish were piranhas. Later he told me how they watched the sonar screen for torpedoes in the water.)

Jan 20, 1991
Dear Mom,
     We're in the southern Gulf area. Air Force is still bombing. We may do an amphibious landing in a couple of weeks. Other than that, just sitting here. We've been intercepting CNN's telecasts back to the states so every now & then we find out what's going on. . . . I hate being on the boat. I, at least, wish we were on the land. . . . David

THE SHAPE OF COLD

Part One

December 23, I drove from St. Paul to Kansas City to spend Christmas with my family. Usually a 6½ hour trip, it took nearly ten hours driving forty miles an hour where I would have gone seventy or seventy-five. Several times I felt the back wheels slide, but somehow the car righted itself again. At times, there were white-out conditions; not from new snow, but from crosswinds driving existing snow horizontally from the fields across the highway. There were streams of blowing snow, west to east on I-35 south. I felt like I was crossing a spillway. I felt like the earth was turned on its side.

The sky was hazy. A gray disk of light called a sun dog shone all the way. It was only the second time I had seen a parhelion, a bright circular band, or halo, around the sun that somehow splits the one sun into three: the greater sun in the center, a smaller sun on each side of the solar halo, the mock suns, the sun dog.

If cold had a form, it would be round, the way someone lost in a blizzard circles. The way the sun through frozen particles in the air forms a parhelic ring.

On the trip I watched the snowbanks that edged the highway where wind lifted veils of snow from the west. Geography was there—a bedrock of land. Yet there was a moving geography over the flat, map-drawer of fields. In that split of *place,* I saw land as change, as return to a point which point had changed on return. Geography was enduring, yet geography was the transitory embankments of snow. A migration within a stasis. A momentum and change within a stability.

When the USS *Okinawa* neared San Diego after the 1991 Persian Gulf War, the helicopters flew from the carrier to the land. David, my son, a marine lieutenant at the time, rode in one of those helicopters. He said when he saw the coast of California from the air—there was nothing like it.

Geography is a map of return. A map that is not an end in itself but a pro-cess—a way to what is ahead—the states in an abstract sense—the destinations of knowing how to get there.

Part Two

One of the books I asked for at Christmas was Upton Sinclair's *The Jungle,* which I reread after many years. "So he came to the stockyards, the black volcanoes of smoke and the lowing cattle and the stench." The packinghouse had been as hard on the men as it was on the cattle.

Bertold Brecht got to it right away in *St. Joan of the Stockyards.* "—the groaning of that steer / Will live forever in my heart." "Who do they think we are? Do they expect us / To stand out here like cattle, ready / For anything?"

Over Christmas, while I was in Kansas City, I made a return trip to the stockyards where my father had come for work in the late 1920s. I drove down the Twelfth Street Viaduct into the stockyards below Kansas City on the bluffs. The old yards are now warehouses, truck yards, and empty lots. One particular corner, on Genessee, is a mound covered with prairie grass and an installation of metal cow-sized cattle, maybe a dozen, as a memorial for the thousands and thousands of cattle that passed through the yards daily.

Further west on Genessee was the West End Hotel and the Kansas City Livestock Exchange, which were surrounded by probably twenty-five acres of pens. It was a geography of violence and turmoil. Fires had trapped animals in their pens. Floods had drowned them. The last flood, in 1951, I was alive to see. I remember the dead pigs floating in the debris. I remember the typhoid shots.

In 1965, the stockyards in Kansas City were razed. My father was then working for Armour in Chicago, but on a return trip to Kansas City, where I lived at the time, I went with him as he looked at the vacant pens and lots, the empty grounds where the Armour plant had stood.

In the old days, before his time, herds had been driven from Texas, Indian Territory, New Mexico, Colorado, and west Kansas to the Santa Fe or Union Pacific railroads in Abilene or Baxter Springs, and later Wichita, Newton, and Dodge City. After a day's ride to Kansas City, the cattle were watered, fed, and loaded again to St. Louis, Chicago, and farther east to be slaughtered. After the cattlemen grew tired of paying yardage charges and feed bills, the Kansas City stockyards were established at the foot of Twelfth Street in the West Bottoms, over old Osage Indian camps near the confluence of the Kaw and Missouri Rivers. The Armour brothers had begun building their meatpacking plants in Chicago, New York, and Kansas City sometime after the Civil War.

I could still almost smell the cattle yards as I drove through the bottoms.

All those years, I was in our house far away from the killing floors of the stockyards, though the smell of it came into the house each night with my father.

From the beginning, there was a history of strife. Farmers fought the drovers who brought cattle sick with Texas fever to their farm cows. Then there were the unions and strikes, the child labor laws, government inspectors, the eventual antitrust suit against Dial Soap. Year after year there were the slit throats of pigs and sheep, the steers stunned with a hammer blow.

"The idea of hanging a carcass on a moving chain and passing it before cutters, each of whom would remove a part or parts, made meat cutting a straight line continuous process" (*Armour and His Time,* Harper Leech and John C. Carroll, Appleton-Century Company, New York, 1938).

On the other end, the animals came out as cuts of meat, canned beef, and pork (Spam), lard, fertilizer, and other byproducts. In the geographies of memory, the railroad yards, quarantine yards, chutes, pens, packinghouse, chimneys, meat lockers, and finally, refrigeration trucks, still operate.

The meatpacking industry is now decentralized in feedlots located across the Great Plains, where the cattle are raised, killed, and processed in one place, then the carcasses are shipped for consumption. Though the old packinghouses are gone, the brutality is still there in the feedlots, the hog barns, and the chicken barns I pass as I travel across the plains. There is still the bloody dismemberment and disembowelment. There is still the geography of survival, the hunt and kill, the great workings of the world. It is now a matter of how economically it can be done.

My father began work by running the elevator in the Armour plant in Kansas City; then he moved on to offals, then other departments, and the second time he worked in the Kansas City plant, after he had been transferred several times to plants in other cities, he eventually became plant superintendent. My father later would die by the surgeon's knife at the age of sixty-two; something in his gut that surgery didn't cure but exacerbated. There was no buffer zone. It was war on the animals, and the animals always lost. It was war on the men, both management and workers. It seems everyone lost to some degree. I remember the bloodstained aprons of the men in the cafeteria during the summer I worked in the stockyards, until I had to quit because of a complaint of nepotism. The cafeteria was on the front lines of war. It was a break, a brief respite between attacks, before they got back to the killing.

No potholders here.

Across the Kaw, west of Kansas City on the bluffs, were the Polish and Slavic communities, the Catholic and Orthodox churches on the hill. Christ was over the stockyards and the steaming cattle and hog pits of the world.

With the money I earned the summer I worked in the order-supply department, I bought a small-faced Bulova that still works and a typewriter on which I began to write.

This is for the memory of my father, Lewis Hall, in his grave in a cemetery on a hill from which downtown Kansas City can be seen. This is for his three-week-old great-grandson beside me, asleep for the moment but starting to stir.

The Colors of Nature: Culture, Identity and the Natural World, edited by Alison Deming and Lauret Savoy, Milkweed Editions, Minneapolis, 2002, for "Slowly Turning Nature."

Witness: Animals in America, Vol. 15, No. 2, 2001, for "Hog Barn." Gratefulness to Simpson College, Indianaola, Iowa, for a first reading of the piece.

A Place in Time, edited by Bret Lott and Scott Olsen, University of Utah Press, 2001, for "July."

Christianity and the Arts, Chicago, Illinois, Fall 2000, for "Transmotion." Gratefulness to the Glen Workshop, St. John's College, Santa Fe, New Mexico, August, 2000, for a first reading of the piece.

Wise Women: Reflections of Teachers at Mid-Life, edited by Phyllis Freeman and Jan Zlotnik Schmidt, Routledge, 2000, for "Mud Ponies."

Modern Fiction Studies, published for Purdue University by Johns Hopkins University Press, Baltimore, Maryland, Vol. 45, No. 1, Spring 1999, for "In-between Places" under the title "Give Me Land, Lots of Land."

The Hungry Mind Review, St. Paul, Minnesota, Spring 1998, for "When the Boats Arrived."

Acknowledgment to Macalester College for a Wallace Travel Grant to China from which "Terra-Cotta Horses" was written.

ACKNOWLEDGMENTS

Diane Glancy teaches Native American literature and creative writing at Macalester College in St. Paul, Minnesota. In 2003 she published *Stone Heart: a Novel of Sacajawea*. She is the recipient of a National Endowment for the Arts, an Oklahoma Book Award, a Minnesota Book Award, an American Book Award from the Before Columbus Foundation, and the Native American Prose Award. Her previous collections of essays are *The Cold-and-Hunger Dance*, *The West Pole*, and *Claiming Breath*. Glancy also published a collection of poetry, *The Shadow's Horse*, with the University of Arizona Press. She won the 2003 Juniper Prize from the University of Massachusetts Press for another collection of poems, *Primer of the Obsolete*. She lives in St. Paul, Minnesota, and Prairie Village, Kansas.

ABOUT THE AUTHOR